MIDMEN

The Modern Man's Guide to Surviving Midlife Crisis

Steve Ochs GED

ISBN: 1499781865
ISBN 13: 9781499781861
Library of Congress Control Number: 2014910383
CreateSpace Independent Publishing Platform
North Charleston, South Carolina

ALSO BY STEVE OCHS

Why Everyone Hates You (Pinnacle)

National Lampoon Jokes, Jokes, Jokes,
Collegiate Edition (National Lampoon)

National Lampoon Jokes, Jokes, Jokes,
Verbal Abuse Edition (National Lampoon)

MIDMEN

The Modern Man's Guide to Surviving Midlife Crisis

For Logothetis Gravatas;
you know what you did.

TABLE OF CONTENTS

ACKNOWLEDGMENTS

First and foremost, thanks to my wife and primary noun, Julie; she is the most important person, place or thing in my life and without her not only wouldn't there be a book, there wouldn't have been a basis for one. Why then, one might wonder, did I not simply dedicate the damn thing to her? And who the hell is Logothetis Gravatas and why did *he* grab the gold ring of dedication? I met my wife twenty-five years ago while working at a comedy club in Detroit. When I was prepared to make permanent our temporary flirtation, she was gone and I had no contact information. To provide me with her info, Logothetis Gravatas, who was the manager at the club, "happened" into the locked, private files of what were believed to be some respectably dangerous club owners. Logothetis is, at the time of this writing, 88-years-old and one of my dearest friends. I can think of no better way to communicate my undying appreciation for his brave act than to dedicate this, a book that would not exist otherwise, to him. But, let's get real, Logi; this is totally for Julie.

My family has been treating me like a star since I performed my first ventriloquist routine at a Boy Scout Blue and Gold dinner when I was seven. Mom, Lloyd, Lori; you've always been certain I was capable of being successful at anything. I doubt this book will go any further toward proving you right than any of my other hair-brained projects, but it wouldn't exist if you didn't stubbornly believe in me.

The anecdotes in MIDMEN are inhabited by composite versions of people I actually know or have known. Much about them has been changed to protect not only the innocent, but also a writer clearly guilty of character assassination. Obviously, I can't thank the people I have grotesqued by name, but you know who you are, you just can't prove it in a court of law.

I knew I needed an editor because just after writing the first half of the book, my computer took on a strange virus. It seemed every time I typed more than four words in a row it jammed my head up my ass. Having cut my writing teeth on TV shows, I wasn't used to being my own boss; I was used to copious notes, verbal abuse and, occasionally, corporal punishment. I needed a boss. Since no one was about to hire me to write MIDMEN, I had to hire someone to hire me. My editor, Lori Stone Handleman is someone I've literally never met in person. I was looking on line and the very first editor I stumbled upon embodied all of the qualities I required. She is the appropriate age and married to a man of the appropriate age, she holds a doctorate in psychology and her resume includes work at the Oxford University Press acquiring psychology and related titles. But most importantly, when we exchanged pictures, in hers she was bathing an elephant in Sri Lanka. She had me at the elephant. My desire to sit in a room alone and write got the project started, but bringing in Lori got it finished and that is much appreciated.

Paul Provenza honored me by saying he would be honored to write my forward. That's a lot of honor, no? He was my dream choice for the task for several reasons. His TV series *Greenroom with Paul Provenza*, his must-read book *¡Satiristas!: Comedians, Contrarians, Raconteurs & Vulgarians* and now legendary cult film *The Aristocrats* all helped pave the way for the kind of honesty and vulgarity that I hope I brought to this book. He is also a fellow veteran stand up comic, a truly decent human being and ultimately empathetic. I'm proud to have his name on the cover with my own.

When writing a book, especially one that purports to place me in the heady, "You should live like me," stratosphere, the number of people whose influence should be acknowledged is very high (as are, coincidentally, several of the people themselves). There are the people who nurtured me, extended my comfort zones, did things that I envied that drove me forward, served as models of integrity, models of diligence, models of empathy, models of swimwear and/or literally outright helped me. Some of them are: Stephen Marks, David Doyle, Charles Dayton, Joey Kola, Julie Weintraub Kreiger, Kitty Martini, Dr. Jackson Varady, Dave Edison, Trisha Cohen, Hila Assifi, Aaron Alberts, Sophie Venable, Scott Buckwald, Melvin George II, Randy Levin, Karen Lee Cohen, Chris Bonno, Luba, John Weiss, Matthew Quinn, Jack Swersie, Russel Roehling and Jim Myers.

FORWARD BY PAUL PROVENZA

Albert Einstein published his paradigm-shifting theory of relativity at age 25. At 25, Pablo Picasso painted his ground-breaking modern art masterpiece, *Les Demoiselles d'Avignon*. Bruce Springsteen was 25 years old when he created his rock and roll masterwork, *Born To Run*. What a bunch of show-offs.

I'm now more than twice that age and I haven't even picked up some dry cleaning that's been ready since I was 25. It's on my "To Do" list but I just haven't gotten around to it yet. The real problem is that my "To Do" list is rapidly becoming my "Bucket List."

Time really does fly when it's no longer on your side. Mick Jagger may still sing about time being on his side, but he's now doing it in a Lycra jumpsuit developed by NASA to hold his wrinkled, jumping jack flesh approximately in place - making the whole spectacle far too ironic. He's now in his 70's and *still* ain't got no satisfaction, so time is clearly not on Mick's side now.

Time never has been on his or anyone else's side. Time is only out for itself. Time's sole purpose is to destroy us. Like a slow-motion flesh eating virus, time devours us whole. From the moment we're born we are actively engaged in the process of dying. And it's only for the *luckiest* among us that it's a really long, slow, lingering death. I know that sucks as a daily affirmation, but it's true.

But they say that with age comes wisdom, and being on the outer edges of middle-aged I'd certainly *like* to believe that's true. But I'm certain someone old came up with that, so it feels to me a little too self-serving. It's increasingly harder for me to believe I'm getting any wiser as the world around me changes more quickly than the arrival of the next iOS upgrade. The technological explosion happening during my middle age is changing the world more profoundly and quickly than it has for any previous generation, and the rate of that acceleration itself is accelerating. My generation is the first whose offspring have a better understanding of technology and the world around them than their parents do. My parents never needed my help understanding a goddamn thing, ever - but the average middle-aged parents now have to ask their prepubescent kids to explain something new to them on a daily basis - usually they're things that were unimaginable to us until about last month. I have no children of my own, so I myself am often reduced to cruising schoolyards with fruit roll-ups and a PS3 trying to lure 13-year-olds home with me just to get some I.T. help.

It's become impossible for me to deny the feeling that no matter how much I may have accomplished in my life, with each day I move further and further away from any kind of relevance to the world around me. It's as if the coach has decided to take me out of the game of life. More and more I feel like I'm just a spectator, being moved higher and higher into the nosebleed section. Any day now I won't even be able to see the game anymore and I'll just be wandering around in the parking lot trying to remember where the hell I left the damned car.

Ironically, my generation has been behaving like children far longer than any generation before us has. I bet you've got little toys in your workspace, don't you? And you know you play air guitar if you're in the car alone and Metallica comes on, don't deny it. My age group is so much about refusing to grow up that as a generation we've decided that 40 is now 30, and 50 now equals 40. We just declared it so - physics, math and time/space continuum be damned. While that suggests that we actually may have *some* degree of control over this whole growing older thing, it's important to remember that there is a very fine line between self-actualization and self-delusion.

That's where this book comes in. What Steve Ochs does here is not deny that 40 really is still 40, and while 50 may now feel to us like 40 used to, he refuses to ignore the truth that it's still got 10 more years of wear on the tires. *"It's going to suck"* is the flat out reality of middle age that Steve solidly embraces as he helps us find the tools within ourselves to make it suck a lot less than it needs to. The wisdom that he has acquired is one that comes from the cold, hard truth that no matter how much the externals of our lives suck, we tend to live oblivious to the fact that we ourselves are responsible for making it *really* suck that much more. With great humor and empathy, Steve distills most of what's challenging in middle age down to recognizing and solving the problems we create for ourselves over and over again, day in and day out. Despite the title, this is a book 25-year-olds should read. It really would save them a lot of aggravation on the way to middle age.

Occasionally, someone younger than I will have heard that whole "wisdom comes with age" thing, and having presumed it's true, will ask me for some kind of advice about how to navigate a life for at least as long as I have. I always answer with the best advice I feel I can ever give anyone who foolishly asks me for advice, which is: "Never listen to anyone's advice." Now I feel I need to amend that with "... Anyone's but Steve Ochs'."

Paul Provenza

PREFACE

"Wisdom doesn't necessarily come with age. Sometimes age just shows up all by itself."

Tom Wilson

I tried Viagra. The results were as shocking to me as they were to everyone else in the room. I have since tried it several more times, but less for shock than for awe. At some point I will have to switch from saying, "I tried Viagra" to "I use Viagra." That time has not yet arrived, as I do not yet *need* Viagra. I can do just fine on my own. But having tried the stuff, I have learned an important lesson: I am an aging man. And what part of me would more quickly categorize me as a man, aging or otherwise, than my sex organ?

Here's how my Viagra adventure unfolded. I was hanging out with a friend of mine. This is one of those close friends you occasionally regret having grown so close to. Not because he's a bad guy but because his TMI gasket is blown. For instance, if he started his day with a great bowel movement he would invite you to celebrate it with him. I'm sorry but I feel stupid and gross high fiving somebody over the size and consistency of their stool. This is the kind of guy who burps rhapsodically in my face and then throws me a 'What do you think of *that*?' look. What do I think of that? I think you need to see a gastroenterologist. I think you're dying inside, that's what I think of that. So I'm hanging out with this friend of mine and he goes through the postmortem of his bodily functions and then leans in and whispers, "Three times last night." He's 55, so I assumed that was how many times he got up to pee. That's nothing to be ashamed of, but it's hardly something to brag about.

I was wrong. He had sex with his wife three times. My first thought was, why did he think it was okay to broadcast his morning shit report to the world but felt compelled to hush himself to talk about sex? The next thing I thought was, so what? I don't even *want* to have sex three times in one night. Maybe I'm doing it wrong, but once feels like plenty. Hey, maybe I'm doing it *right*! Maybe he had sex three times last night and sucked at it every time. Maybe his wife was in the middle of a hot flash thinking, *Not again!*

It's not like my wife and I are sex-starved. We still have regular sex… well, we still have sex regularly. There is a distinction. The other day a friend my age asked me if my wife and I have sex often. I said, "What do you mean by often?" and he said, "You know, like, ever?" The average middle-aged couple has sex once a week, twice if they also have sex with each other. I haven't really considered doing it more than once in a night for quite a while. Multiple events in a single 24-hour period are generally reserved for lazy, half-drunk afternoons and evenings during our annual beach vacation. At home, my wife and I do it often enough for us. Everybody finds his or her own schedule on that stuff. But then I pictured myself rising up heroically from our bed after number three, my wife dazed, unable to move as I throw her a wink and strut off to the kitchen for a snack. I have to admit I felt jealous.

My friend went on to tell me—unsolicited of course—that the secret to his 55-year-old virility was none other than Viagra. "Hmm," I replied truthfully.

"Do you want one?" my friend asked, digging a finger into the change pocket of his jeans' change pocket and pulling out the much-celebrated blue pill.

"Fuck no!" I snapped, "I don't need that shit! I'm just fine in that department, thank you very much."

But as the days passed I found myself reminiscing about me and my dick and the crazy times we used to have together. It's like looking at old pictures of myself with a full head of hair: bittersweet. I paged through my mental photo album of my dick, watching it rapidly transition from childhood to early adolescence, all over the course of a single viewing of *Barbarella*. Teenage me following my dick toward females like a man stranded in the desert following his divining rod toward water. Then I flashed back to the actual sexual relationships I was lucky enough to have from my teens right through my 20s, and remembered that pretty much all of them included repeat daily performances. I was a dynamo, I was a Gatling gun of love, cranking hard, firing in flurries, ejecting spent cartridges, blowing the smoke off the tip and loading new rounds. Somehow over the years I had traded down to a pump-action single-shot. Was my sex organ just a reflection of my whole body, aging in its own way, its posture stooping and its strength diminishing? I totally got that my frequency had diminished, but I hadn't begun to consider the possibility that my erections might be weakening. It wasn't obvious. It's like realizing that the hour hand on my trouser clock had quietly moved from 1:00 to 3:00 and never noticing that I don't see 1:00 anymore. I was ready to try the pill, but I was *not* ready to ask my douchey friend for one of his. There were other sources.

My penis has been getting more email than me since I bought my first computer. Somewhere out in the digital ether there are millions of companies that seem to have a beef with my jerky. A million of them think it's not big enough and would like to be entrusted with its enlargement. Another million can't stand by watching idly while I ejaculate prematurely, though that image does make for quite a visual. But most of these millions of mysterious advocates for my under-sized, hair-triggered junk simply don't like my erections. They don't seem to believe I can fully achieve one without proper counsel and treatment. They want their licensed doctor to examine my faulty tower via an online form and make the sound medical decision that'll get me the help I so desperately need. These angels of trouser mercy send my penis emails from all over the world, though they're mostly from countries known for laws as lax as they assume my erections to be.

Taking a lap through the house to locate my never-where-I-left-them reading glasses, the fucking things must be possessed, and stealing a private moment at my computer, I directed my advanced Googling techniques toward the task of finding an acceptable online pharmacy. Again, there are literally thousands of them and not only do they not trust me with the stewardship of my own erection, they can't agree on prices. I finally land on a "pharmacy" in "Canada." My cross-referencing indicated that the service was as reputable as these things can be. Since, according to *Forbes Magazine* (the ED paper of record), 77% of Viagra sold through these channels is fake with plaster as a binding agent and printer ink supplying the blue, this choice is important. Had I known the risks, I would simply have asked my doctor for a prescription. Anyway, I filled out a form all but bereft of personal questions and ordered the minimum, which turned out to be enough pills to keep me hard until rigor mortis takes over the job.

When the pills arrived a week or so later I happened to be home alone so I decided to keep the purchase a secret. What better way to measure just how radical the change might be than to spring it, as it were, on my wife? The pills themselves were *not* authentic Viagra; they were the generic, *Sildenafil* citrate, manufactured in India. It's the same chemical sold as Viagra and it's also used to treat pulmonary arterial hypertension so I guess you can also get a *heart on*. Thank you. I'll be here all book. I would have preferred the real thing, or at least a counterfeit with a knock-off logo, but since I have an entire misspent youth of amateur drug testing behind me, I tried them anyway. The pills came with a plastic pill-splitting device. It seems you can't take an entire pill or the effects would be so strong your entire body would be rendered as stiff as a weight-bearing stud; no more sitting, you'd have to be rolled to a wall on a hand truck and leaned. Now all I had to do was find an opportunity to use the stuff.

My wife was enduring something I didn't know about until it emptied its travel bag and moved into my house. It's the age-related travails of something called perimenopause. This little jackpot is the precursor to actual menopause. It's a transitional period (pun intended) where she goes from regular cycles to crazy erratic periods, sort-of-periods and pre-sort-of-periods. I will say in her defense that were I enduring this roller coaster of hormonally infused bullshit I would not be the most agreeable fucker in the world either. I'll delve way deeper into the dynamics of the menopausal household later in Chapter Three, "The Radius," but for now, suffice it to say we have our good days and our bad days. Because "peri" bad days start a few days before *real* bad days, we had to develop a code to communicate where things are at. This is mostly because the question, "Are you pre-menstrual?" is famously punishable by death. So, to communicate the current state of affairs wordlessly we enlisted the help of a small refrigerator magnet of a Rasta saying, "No Problem, Mon." Now I needn't speak the forbidden words, I can simply check the side of the fridge. When the Rasta is upright, he speaks the truth. When he is upside down, "Big Problem, Mon."

One golden afternoon I was on my way to the gym and saw that the Rasta was ready to party. I called my wife to see if tonight felt like a "date night." More code. Work it out, Sherlock. She reminded me that her mother was coming to visit, but shouldn't arrive until after midnight, so, "No problem, Mon." A touch nervous about what to expect from the ersatz Viagra, I dropped half of one into my shorts pocket and headed out. Since the pill is supposed to take about an hour to take effect, with the effects lasting around four hours, I figured I would take it while I was still at the gym and by the time I got home and we settled in and had a drink or whatever, my Canadian/Indian, Viagra/*Sildenafil* citrate should be ready to bring its Fuckenstein monster to life.

I hit the gym, worked out for a while, popped the pill, worked out for a little while longer and then hit the shower. It was a good work-out and the shower felt great. Seriously, the shower felt really nice. Really, really nice. Oh shit. *Come on!* It had only been about 20 minutes but the pill was, to say the least, working. Holy shit! Nature may have dropped my trouser clock to 3:00 but half a pill and 20 minutes later it was high noon. The good news was that the showers at my gym are in individual stalls. The bad news was the towels are kept at the end of the line of showers and I was about four stalls in. There was no way I could possibly take the walk to get my towel without making a lot of enemies . . . or some unwanted friends. I rinsed and turned off the water, hoping the lack of stimulation would allow things to drop into repose. Nothing. Viagra, or whatever that shit was, lives up to its hype. Operative word: up. I tried thinking about people I loved who died, picturing old friends and grandparents as vividly as I could in my mind. Nothing. It just made my memories of them feel incredibly disrespectful. Having a raging boner while thinking about my dear departed grandmother might be the wrongest thing I've ever done. I turned on the cold water and let it hit me squarely on the problem. Nope, I was kind of digging it. If you have never personally been trapped in a men's locker room shower with an overenthusiastic hard on and nothing to cover it, then count your blessings. It makes you realize just how much more naked your dick is when it's excited. In its normal state, it's kind of, "Okay, nothing to see here, just another dick. Move along." But you throw the blue pill into the mix and it's, "Attention K-Mart shoppers!"

During a rare moment of shower room solitude, I was able to extricate myself from the stall, dress and shuffle out the gym door exhibiting all the finesse of a mime performing the containment of explosive diarrhea.

Finally in the car, I breathed a sigh of relief and pulled out of the lot. I don't know if you took a bus to school when you were, say, 11 or 12, but I distinctly recall that the bumps and turns on the ride to and from, aroused me. I think this was purely physical stimulation because if it were actually a turn-on I would have grown up to be some kind of deviant bus fucker. You'd have found me standing around on street corners waiting to hop on the next bus and "take" it. So here I was at 47 having a total sense memory as I headed down the road driving an automatic *and* a stick.

My cell phone rang and I answered with the Bluetooth. It was my wife telling me she needed me to stop at the store. "But, I—" But nothing, she was cooking a special dinner and needed one clove of garlic, period. Alrighty then.

I pulled into the Ralph's Supermarket parking lot with a plan forming in my head. Having nothing to wear but loose gym shorts, I figured the only semi-decent cover I could offer myself would be a full-size shopping cart. I paused to make another futile attempt at battling the problem with the strength of my mind. I thought about the pain from a recent disc extrusion, nothing. I thought about the haircut I got the day before and how when I used the hand mirror to see the back of my head my bald spot actually flipped me off. Still stiff. Another try at dead grandma? Nope.

Fuck it. I started to slide out of the car. Any movement, however slight, made me feel like I was raping my own shorts. Seeing that the coast was clear, I scurried over to the closest cart and when I was a mere step away some crew cut 20-something in camo swept it up without breaking stride and headed into the store. And there I stood, alone and absolutely arrestable. When I finally got behind a cart I clutched it like a life preserver. Bag of garlic cloves, self-checkout, vamoose.

Finally home, I wondered if my wife would notice if I didn't say anything and just walked into the house with her bag of garlic and a nylon tent pitched in my shorts. I gave it a try.

"Hi honey," I sang as I sidled up next to her at the stove.

"Hello," she said turning to give me a kiss and accidentally bumping into Iron Man. "Oh my god!"

I took a step back and let her take in the full power and glory of my turbo-charged fun stick.

"Honey, I . . ." She couldn't even find the words.

"I know, baby. And it's yours and yours alone."

"Not so much," she said, pointing across the kitchen where her bug-eyed mother was standing next to the refrigerator. "Mom arrived early."

Truth be told, I don't know if the re-setting of my penile-clock is a direct result of physical aging. Should I expect a decrease in testosterone at age 55? Sure. Should I assume that the sexual familiarity of my now 20-year marriage might be contributing to my laissez-faire sex pistol? That's logical. Or could it be nature working in the larger sense, telling me that my services are no longer needed, that my seed should nevermore be planted? Most likely it's a combination of all of the above.

The ravages of age are not restricted to showing themselves on my tallywacker (by the way just knowing that word is a sign of aging). I am aging at the cellular level, the physical level and the social level. I am aging in private, I am aging in public, I am aging in my clothes and aging even faster out of them. But I am far from alone.

There are currently 300 million Americans, give or take 17 million. Seventy-eight million are what we call "Baby Boomers," people born between 1945 and 1964. By 2070 they will all be dead. Right behind them, and aging competitively, is Generation X, people born between the early 1960s and early 1980s, which brings them in at 33 to 52 years old, which places the older half of the group neatly in midlife. That's right fellow Boomers, Gen X, the little fuckers who looked at us like we were old and clueless, are now suffering *with* us! Excuse me while I mix myself a little schadenfreude cocktail. The Xers *and* the Boomers are all realizing that they have fewer years ahead of them than behind them. Half of these people are men and a whole lot of *those* are freaking out. This freaking out phenomenon is commonly called "Midlife Crisis." Its sufferers represent the highest concentration of wealth, the greatest earnings and (drum roll please) the highest rate of suicide. They also represent more than four million embarrassing gold stud earrings, seventeen billion individual hair transplants and eight thousand miles of hairy muffin top. These guys are what I call the MIDMEN.

According to a study published in 2004 by the MacArthur Foundation's Research Network on Successful Midlife Development or *MIDMAC* (seriously, that's what they call it), MIDMEN are one tough crowd to nail down. The study states that 26.8% of adults ages 40-60 report suffering through a midlife crisis, but these may not have been "real" midlife crises. For the purposes of the study, a severe emotional and/or mental reaction to someone close to us dying, our marriage going to shit, or our health failing while we are in our middle years were not included in the definition of midlife crisis. Those are the most common reasons *for* midlife crisis! All that's left after that is graying pubes. I think we can agree that many if not most men experience some degree of crisis-level discomfort as their own rapid aging and inevitable death confronts them.

Because I believe that inciting events like those listed above, as well as empty nest syndrome and "I just got a good look at myself in the wrong mirror" trigger genuine midlife crises, I'm apt to go with an 80% figure.

A MIDMAN turns 50 every 7.2 seconds. Out of roughly 38 million MIDMEN, not one takes his 50th birthday particularly well. Some take it much worse than others. Sadly, men constitute only 37% of the total number of patients in therapy according to a poll published by *Therapy in America*. The rest are out there searching for the answers on their own. They may try to find them in the driver's seat of a powerful sports car, at the bottom of a bottle, or in the hypnotic gyrations of a stripper . . . or frequently all of the above. No case of midlife crisis on record has ever been cured by these techniques, though problems related to having too much money are easily solved by any combination of the three.

The MIDMAN hasn't had sensitivity training but, unlike his father, he was raised in a more liberal society. His father was expected to be the breadwinner and man of the house, but the modern man is all but totally accustomed to a world where women work and men can be homemakers. More men than women are chefs and cooking for the family has become a shared task in many homes. The Laura Petrie 'come fuck me' apron has yet to find its house*husband* equivalent, but rest assured it's coming. Of course we do still have our gender roles. If the car gets a flat, the man on board is still going to be the one who has to get out of the car on a rainy night and fix it (though I can't imagine why he doesn't have AAA). The modern man can cry and not feel like it's a threat to his manliness, which is nice when you're changing a flat tire on a rainy night.

The starkest difference between our middle years and our father's is that while society instructed the MIDMAN's father to be mature at a young age, the MIDMAN was raised in an environment that prizes youthfulness at an "old" age. Men over 30 are already viewed as 'older' by those under 30, but can't consciously accept it and insist on using the word "dude" like a comma. This is understandable. We have to cling to our youth because if we're not who we were, then who *are* we? Surrendering to the fact that we're aging is just the warm-up act for surrendering to death. So we act like it isn't happening. But one day the MIDMAN looks in the mirror and feels like Jeff Goldblum in *The Fly* watching himself pull a tooth out; it's just freaky. The MIDMAN, or MID-DUDE as the case may be, is in a tough spot. He's modern enough to admit to *himself* that he's freaking out, but still directed by society not to appear too vulnerable. He's crushed under the weight of life's pressures—bills, family, health—and is suddenly having a midlife crisis on top of it. He still has another round or two of fight left in him but it's getting a little harder for him to hear the bell. In many cases he has let himself go to shit physically, but even if he's lived a healthy lifestyle, the clock itself is rendering him semi-lame. This is not leaving him in a particularly good mood.

According to Medterms.com, midlife crisis is "a period of personal emotional turmoil and coping challenges that some people encounter when they reach middle age, accompanied by a desire for change in their lives, brought on by fears and anxieties about growing older." The psychoanalyst and social scientist Elliott Jaques introduced the phrase "midlife crisis" in a study of creative geniuses back in 1965. Examining the lives of numerous composers and artists, Dr. Jaques found "abrupt changes in style or declines in productivity about age 35."

Note that back in 1965 Jaques was referring largely to men 35 years old. Today that would seem young, finally proving to some degree that 40 actually is the new 30. Regardless of age, midlife crisis is what occurs when a man reaches his point of no return. This is the time when he stops counting his years up and starts counting them down.

I had my shitty epiphany, or *shitpiphany*, while I was being taken down by that extruding disc between L-4 and L-5 (and we'll get into just how unfortunate it is that you probably know exactly what those medical terms mean later). I was riding a bike, hit a bump and aged 20 years. I had never considered that my body might plan a self-demolition and my mind wouldn't be invited. But there I was at 47 having the realization that this "aging" thing wasn't fucking around. I freaked out. Having been a jack of many trades and never over the top successful at any also cast an eerie glow on the dimming light of my remaining years. Mercifully, regular yoga, a healthy diet and my fortuitous genetic Ashkenazi Jewiness had been holding off visible decay. But when my back went out my mortality calendar started dropping pages like the time-lapse montage in an old noir movie. I started melting down. I didn't know what to do or how to react. I was changed; not a different man necessarily, but a man in a more advanced period of manhood. It was like a midlife Bar Mitzvah; today I am a MIDMAN.

My instinctive reaction to this unexpected *continuing to be alive* problem was to try and solve it. I asked myself the question, "How does a middle-aged man actually enjoy his share of the first half of the 21st century?" First I had to simplify the problem. By process of elimination, I was able to reduce my situation down to three simple truths:

1. I'm actually getting old.
2. It's ultimately going to suck.
3. Tough shit. I will still need to live life to the fullest until I can't anymore.

Within these three truths lies a circuitous path of fears, emotions and physical hardships. This is because entering the transitional MIDMAN period of life is never a single challenge. Every individual MIDMAN has his own unique combination of exclusively personal problems.

PREFACE

Who is a MIDMAN? He's the guy with:

1. A kid blowing a huge tuition bill by spending his days smoking weed and playing video games instead of going to class . . . just like he did!
2. A wife who apparently believes his penis is radioactive and even though she loves him, will not risk radiation poisoning to pleasure him.
3. Kids who moved out just in time for his parents to become the *new* kids and move in.
4. A beer belly staging a total penile eclipse.
5. A seat on the couch in the waiting room of life reading a copy of *Who Gives a Fuck Anymore?* magazine.
6. Exactly enough computer knowledge to collect his email and look at Internet porn.
7. A sizable bet placed on which will go to shit first: his health or the planet.
8. Eyes that can't stop looking at younger women who can't stop not giving a shit.
9. A music collection that goes from Aerosmith all the way to ZZ Top but includes nothing from this century.

I suffered from numbers 6, 7 and 8 along with numerous other problems. I was troubled. I needed solutions to my problems so I set about seeking them out. I like to read so I took to the bookshelves for my answers. It turned out there were precious few books that even attempted to address my situation. I would be lying if I said there were none . . . but there were none. I was thus left with no other choice but to seek out the answers wherever they could be found. My search led me around the world and I gleaned knowledge from sources as disparate as Buddhists in Cambodia to Rastas in Jamaica.

The Rastas were funnier, the Buddhists were more serene, and they both smelled like incense. I even spent time with hospice patients who can be funny and serene . . . and could often benefit from a little incense.

Then I dipped my toe into the heady work of philosophers and thinkers who have attempted to demystify this subject before me, from Carl Jung to Larry David. I thank them for their generosity in sharing their astute observations about this difficult time of life. I will share some of those with you within the pages to follow (read: I plagiarize people who are much smarter than me). As I tossed the different thoughts and contemplations around, concepts and methods began to form that would guide my very personal midlife transition. Light appeared on the horizon.

I had done all this studying and contemplating for all those endless hours, across the thousands of miles, in the hopes that I would find true happiness or at least a night of un-interrupted sleep. The result was that I had no big problem absorbing the truths of items 1 and 2:

1. I'm actually getting old.
2. It's ultimately going to suck.

But item 3, "Tough shit. I will still need to live life to the fullest until I can't anymore," took a little longer. In a moment of enlightenment, I experienced another, even more stirring, epiphany. I came to the realization that notwithstanding diet, exercise and Viagra, I could not change the more dominant physical aspects of aging—not mine, not my parents', not anybody's—but many other factors were actually under my control. My happiness was one of them. It all came down to identifying and acknowledging the things that really mattered to me and making sure those things were well represented in my day-to-day life.

PREFACE

Minimizing the negative aspects of aging, identifying the things that really matter, and adjusting my life to accommodate both was no simple feat. However, I believe I have pulled this off and those who know me well would probably agree. So, imbued with my shiny new wisdom, I set out to explain myself with a one-man theater piece I called *Life in the Middle Ages*.

Choosing to do the show was a natural move given my history. I spent about a decade and a half headlining across the country as a stand-up comic. Clearly the jokes in this book should be better. I'm also the son of a shrink mother and a comic father, so I was constantly exposed to both of their schools of thought.

The show enjoyed an extended run as Best of the Hollywood Fringe for Solo Comedy. The positive reactions of audiences and critics who attended *Life in the Middle Ages* convinced me that I had something helpful to share. By mixing humor with my observations I found that I was actually having a positive effect on others! The hugs (from *men*, I should add) instead of handshakes that I received so frequently after my performances were more encouraging still . . . if occasionally awkward (keep it quick, dude).

MIDMEN: The Modern Man's Guide to Surviving Midlife Crisis is essentially a road map, which is good since, like me, you probably don't ask for directions. It's a do-it-yourself guide to working out your own shit. But advice is like pasta: the sauce you cover it with will dictate the flavor. So why should you want the sauce of my point of view on the pasta of your midlife crisis? And why does that analogy seem so gross and wrong? Truth be told, you can't be shown a way out of your midlife crisis because your circumstances are unique. But you can be given the tools you need to discover your own individual solutions.

There will be references to all manner of writers, studies and statistics as you move through MIDMEN. There will also be some quizzes, polls and write-in questionnaires. My intent is to offer you an informative, maybe even life-enhancing roadmap while at the same time trying to keep you entertained.

I assume that most of the people who read this book will not be doctors or researchers themselves. This is neither a medical journal, the record of an independent study, nor a textbook. My experience in examining numerous books on this subject is that virtually all of them take on a fairly technical tone. This book is for you, the pudgy, the balding, the under-fucked, the emotionally bereft overachiever yearning to acquire a kind of happiness that can't be bought at any price. Beloved American comedian Andy Kindler put it more succinctly than I ever could: "I did some focus groups and I found out that my target audience is men, my age, who are me."

Chapter 1

THE PROBLEM

"If someone has a midlife crisis while playing hide & seek, does he automatically lose because he can't find himself?"

Steven Wright

Shanae used to work in my office. She's about 25. One day I told her I was tired because I hadn't had enough sleep. She said, "I thought older people didn't need as much sleep." Nice.

If my extruding disc hadn't already triggered my midlife crisis when I was 47, her innocent comment could easily have been the swinging foot that kicked me squarely in the balls of reality. You never know what's going to get you. Sometimes midlife crisis is insidious, an unfortunate series of events that are not threatening in and of themselves. Like the way our backs go out, and don't even tell me your back never goes out. Most of the time when a MIDMAN's back goes out, nothing actually happened. Maybe you reached for your shoe or put something in the trunk of the car and—there it goes!

As our bodies age and our social lives adapt, we start collecting little acceptances. We *accept* our backs going out, the aching in our knees as we make our way to the bathroom in the middle of the night, that innocent extra 20, 30 or more pounds that have crept onto our new slowly-metabolizing bodies. We accept that we are not receiving the kind of attention from the opposite sex we once did. But one day, out of nowhere it hits us for reals and we age an entire lifetime. We are instantly subject to the rules of mortality. We're like an ancient vampire getting caught in a ray of sunshine; the centuries liberated, our physical infallibility melts away as we claw at the air theatrically. We begin envying our pets' or our children's ignorance. More precisely, we envy the ignorance of anyone or anything that enjoys the privilege of living their life without the certainty of their own fleshy obsolescence following them around like a stalker.

Though my traitorous back had already triggered my midlife crisis, it was the process of meticulously going over my estate, signing a living will and creating a trust that really sealed the crisis into the Tupperware bowl of my life and burped it. Yes, I planned my own funeral, even laying out clear instructions for where I would like to have my ashes spread – which would be the floor of an auto parts shop that now sits where my favorite Long Island, NY rock club, Ubies OTJ's, used to be (hallowed ground; I did lighting for The Ramones there).

What I was actually doing was using the busy work of preparing for my suddenly very inevitable death to avoid confronting the emotional aspects of it. Avoidance is a perfectly valid technique for dealing with this situation, but we'll get into that later. Once all that work was done and my affairs were in order, my mind was freed up to assess the situation in a more immediate way. So, I turned to the physical. If some part of me was going to turn out the lights on my little life party, I wasn't going to let it sneak up on me. I got checked up, colonoscopied, scanned and bled. Every doctor assured me that I was as healthy as could be and that I really needed to stop being so paranoid. So now I had lost both the distractions of getting my paperwork in order and of clearing myself physically. There was no place else to go but into my mind. Midlife crisis, it turns out, is much less about a loss of flesh and far more about a loss of innocence, the stripping-away of the illusion of choice and order.

For me the attack of the alien thoughts came from two directions: one, that my time was limited but I didn't know just how limited, and two, that my life while I am alive really counts. Any second could be my last. Was I using this precious time properly? If I were literally lying on my deathbed reviewing my life, would I feel like I had lived it well? Did I have a clear idea of what actually mattered to me? Did I remember to turn off the toaster oven? And the toughest question: was I actually *capable* of living a life I'd be proud of in my final moments? By that standard the answer would be no. I was far too obsessed with the fact that life was passing by as fast as if it had an A.C.M.E. rocket on its back for me to actually live.

In most cases, the moment of midlife crisis inception isn't obvious. It comes on slowly like a summer head cold; both make you want to crawl back into bed and take pills. My personal situation would have to be described as a combination of slow ramp up topped off by my shitpiphany. It can't be traced to a major disease or a thoughtless remark from, let's say, *Shanae*. Just years of hair loss chipping away at my youthful appearance, wrinkles slowly etching onto my face, a subtly decreasing libido, and then that disc extrusion between L3 and L4. Pain is a brilliant teacher; it commands you to pay attention to the lesson. And when the quiz includes questions like, "Do I really want to live if it's going to hurt this bad?" you've really got to consider your answers. Wrinkles, hair, sex life and the other key components of aging can all sit together at the midlife crisis conference table, but the meeting can't really begin until mortality and quality of life sit down.

Elliott Jaques may have been the scholar who actually came up with the term midlife crisis, but it didn't become the generic Jell-O or Kleenex term for explaining why your dad was such a dick until the late 70s. Jaques was interested in what are called "critical phases," which are stages of transition. He dubbed the critical phase that occurs around age 35 (remember: 45 is the new 35, seriously) "Midlife Crisis" and Harley Davidson dealerships have been sending him commission checks ever since. Before then, this passage was referred to as "male climacteric," which, as you can tell by the root word climax, refers to our sexuality. And not in a particularly welcome way, either. Male *climacteric*. Apparently, Jaques came to understand that in midlife crisis, making loud noises every time you sit down or get up in the living room probably means you're making fewer loud noises in the bedroom.

Carl Jung was born in Switzerland in 1875 and thanks to the crisp, cold air and a healthy diet he is only now experiencing his midlife crisis. I'm kidding of course; he died in 1961 but before doing so the great man had a mega-midlife crisis that led him to concepts that can benefit us to this day.

Jung had this to say about the transition we now know as midlife: "The knowledge that one day we must surely die is one of the most disagreeable discoveries of childhood, but there are a number of ego-defense mechanisms at our disposal to take the sting out of the dreadful truth and for the first forty years, the thought that old age is far off and death too remote to bear worrying about. Then, suddenly, the realization dawns that it is not such a long way off after all – in fact, it is rushing up towards us one like the ground toward a complacent parachutist." Good times.

The speed at which we feel the future hurling toward us is largely established by the speed at which we see the past vanishing behind us. I'm talking about when we say shit like, "That was three years ago!? Get the fuck out of here!" Our mind is often blown by how fast time passed since a particular event and, because we humans enjoy the gift of involuntary deductive reasoning, our logic builds on that fact and surmises that the next time period of the same length will zip by just as quickly. So, we project further and the next thing you know we've convinced ourselves that we'll be dying of old age in a time span that will feel like a long lunch. When I have a birthday I am always amazed how fast it came around. I actually have to rehearse for my next age number before it arrives so I don't get whiplash when my birthday hits. So, as I write I am freshly 55, but I'm already rehearsing in my mind for 56. And when I'm 56 I will try on 57, etc. etc. Maybe I should just skip all the way ahead and consider my age as dead. I'm dead years old. However, unlike the numbered, living years, my deadth birthday is the one I won't feel.

Midlife crisis doesn't offer firm criteria for diagnosis; it just overtakes you while you're busy being young and immortal, and then lies on you like a narcoleptic hooker. It introduces itself to you in the bathroom in the middle of the night, or the fitting room mirror of a department store when the fluorescent lights illuminate every line, wrinkle or newly etched imperfection in your face.

Midlife crisis is the stark understanding that the promise of death waits behind the slow torture of living decomposition. It is the moment when you turn your observation of the people aging around you back on yourself.

According to Carl Jung (and me, if his word isn't good enough for you), we are actually predisposed to survive our midlife transition. Of course this seems like good news, but then we are also predisposed to heal after receiving third degree burns and that doesn't make the unspeakable pain any easier. Jung presents a rosy post-MIDMAN era in his list of five main phases of midlife:

1. Accommodation (meeting others' expectations; actually, this takes place in the first part of life, but is the context in which midlife processes take place)
2. Separation (rejecting the accommodated self)
3. Liminality (a period of uncertainty, where life seems directionless and meandering)
4. Reintegration (working out 'who I am' and becoming comfortable with that identity)
5. Individuation (facing up to and accepting the undesirable aspects of our own character)

We needn't analyze the list phase-by-phase right now because the third phase really pegs the mental state of the MIDMAN. Jung's "liminality" is essentially a way to describe the crossroads in our lives where we stop and assess our situation, usually involuntarily. If we are reasonably sane, we're aware of whether we're happy with our life predicament. If we're unsatisfied, we face a complicated period of determining how we will face our future and process our past. Even if we're extremely happy in our lives, liminality will pay us a visit. Freud described adolescence as an expression of "torturous psychosexual conflict." MIDMEN in the throes of liminality describe adolescence as "a fucking picnic." If we compare midlife crisis to a war, then liminality is the point at which we acknowledge that we are under siege. Once the mind starts to fixate on mortality and finality we have to make some big decisions or prepare to shut down completely, which is an option that is all too frequently exercised.

Jung writes about a businessman who, at 45, finds he is able to retire, so he does . . . but he has no other plans! So he gets bored and feels ill. Suddenly with nothing to do but think, the businessman is in this period of liminality. When he had his business, he never needed to ask himself what mattered or explore his priorities. He was too busy trying to transfer money from other people's pockets into his own. Then *kaboom*, money fell into second place behind the preservation of his own ass. This is much like my finalizing my will and obsessing over my health; both are distractions from the matter at hand.

But take heart (or heart medications, or at least a baby aspirin); you can enjoy your future and, indeed, even get a few laughs out of your midlife crisis if you make the effort to get yourself in the right frame of mind. Spoiler alert: I'm over mine! The first step is to know the enemy by establishing the basis of your unique personal midlife crisis.

Chapter 2

THE REASON

"Always remember that you are absolutely unique. Just like everyone else."

Margaret Mead

No two midlife crises are exactly alike. They're just like Daniel Day Lewis' acting roles, only less intense. However, just like the physical manifestations of middle age, there are some components of midlife crisis that most MIDMEN share to one degree or another. The prominence or intensity of a given component will shade the way your midlife crisis impacts you.

If you live in a country that enjoys what we know as western civilization, that being jobs, schools, bills, families, restaurants, trash pickup, mass Smartphone hypnosis, etc., the cause of your midlife crisis is probably pretty predictable. For your convenience, I have identified the top five likely reasons. You will no doubt see yourself and your situation in one or more of these. If you see yourself in all five, that is some fucked up shit. I will come back to these later in the book and deliver viable solutions for each.

1. The Seven-Year Itch. Most people, men and women, assume that the majority of midlife crises are initiated by what is commonly referred to as the "Seven Year Itch," though for MIDMEN this would more appropriately be called the "Twenty Year-ish Itch." The term basically means that a man in a relationship, generally a marriage, finds that after several years he wants something else out of life. He becomes agitated and restless and starts eyeballing (or literally balling) younger women. While this is a classic symptom of midlife crisis, it is certainly not exclusive to MIDMEN. According to Alfred Kinsey, a human sexuality researcher whose 1948 publication "Sexual Behavior in the Human Male" was one of the first recorded works to address human sexual behavior, approximately 20-25% of men engage in extramarital sex at least once during their marriage. However, a study at the New England Research Institute showed that just 2% out of more than 1,700 MIDMAN-aged guys reported doing someone other than their wife. So the whole young blond and sports car thing is a bit exaggerated. Chris Rock famously said, "*A man* is only as *faithful as his* options." I'm not sure that's entirely true, but it's not far off. Most MIDMEN are protected from making a terrible moral mistake by their natural lack of desirability.

The MIDMAN's desire to get him some strange often has no bearing on the strength of his marriage. In cases where the relationship is by all standards great and the guy *still* gets the itch, his wife or significant other gets pretty damn confused. It's almost impossible for a partner to accept that chemicals and nature are manifesting themselves in their loved one in such a counterintuitive, counterproductive way. If you've ever had teenagers in the house you should have some understanding of how the human lab can create a monster.

Of course he wants to have sex with new and frequently younger women; everyone wants to have sex with new young women! Shit, half the *women* I know who are in long-lasting relationships wouldn't mind having sex with new, young women, but this isn't about the sex itself. For the MIDMAN it's about restoring a sense of youth. Looking at younger women and knowing you are no longer on their "things to do" list is very difficult for men. Women experience a very similar thing and even have similar infidelity statistics, but they have a different understanding of the situation. That's because they already have a million books like this one.

I would be hard-pressed to believe that any man would opt to put the peace and normalcy of his monogamous life in jeopardy for no more than an awesome sex session. Unless he is a simpleton, he knows that getting an orgasm, no matter how *swear at the top of your lungs, jerk around like you're suffering an epileptic seizure*-awesome it might be, is not worth it. But the penis has a huge ego of its own, and it's the penis' ego that does the thinking when MIDMEN stray during their midlife crisis. MIDMEN whose midlife crises center on an affair (prostitutes and strip club visits count as affairs if you're doing them without a hall pass) are probably not just doing it for new and improved orgasms; they're doing it to try and re-establish the youthful, sexual identity they once had. Men who have never had a go at anyone other than their own partner also suffer from this need; they're just more honorable. The good news is, if the guy sticks it out for a couple of years (do your own joke) the itch will subside and he can often return to enjoying the comfort, support and mutual growth of a healthy marriage.

2. Low T. "Low T" is more than just my rapper name (limp rhymes with pimp, yo), it's also the cause of what is called male menopause. Though male menopause is a term frequently misused as another way to say midlife crisis, they are not the same thing, though a guy can suffer from both. Frankly, men can also suffer from *menopause* if they're living with a woman who's going though it! According to the Mayo Clinic, male menopause or *andropause* is when a man's hormone production and testosterone bioavailability slowly drop off. When this happens, the guy may notice changes like erectile dysfunction, low energy or shitty attitude. Then one day while acting pissy and not being in the mood for sex or even masturbation, the guy realizes that he is experiencing all the other signs of aging and that none of the process is reversible. . . *then* he has a midlife crisis. A man could, conceivably, go for a long period of time not noticing the symptoms of andropause and not be bothered in the least. But if the symptoms act as a catalyst, causing him to acknowledge his inevitable physical obsolescence, then my friend, that feller has got him a USDA prime choice midlife crisis.

So how can you tell if low testosterone is factoring into your feelings and behavior? Again, the Mayo Clinic lays it out:

Changes in sexual function. If you based it on the number of TV commercials, you'd think more guys have erectile dysfunction than cars. Of course that's not the case, but lots of MIDMEN will notice reduced sexual desire, fewer erections (including during sleep and while driving on bumpy roads), less youthful erections and even infertility. The testes might also become smaller, which could not possibly be more symbolically horrifying.

Changes in sleep patterns. Low testosterone can fuck with your sleep. But how would you know? You might just be lying awake thinking about your shrinking balls.

Physical changes. That body fat you put on? It could be age-related. Aging will also reduce your muscle bulk, reduce your endurance and decrease your bone density. But wait, there's more; how about swollen, tender breasts? Isn't that great, you finally get a pair of sensitive tits you can play with anytime you want, but not only aren't you horny enough to care, they're *your tits*!

Emotional changes. The changes listed above creep up so slowly you may not notice them individually, so acknowledging them may not be the reason for your foul mood. Low testosterone may be working behind the scenes to decrease your motivation or self-confidence. This chemically bums you out and screws with your concentration and your memory. Plus your balls shrink. Did I already mention that? Sorry, I have trouble concentrating and remembering things.

3. Major Loss (human). Widowers are especially vulnerable to terrible midlife crises because of the volatile mixture of their sudden awareness of finality and their deep loss. They lose not just a person but also a partner, an appendage. The term "interdependent" is often used to describe a couple's unhealthy reliance on one another, but interdependence is at the very core of the healthiest relationships. Think about it; everyone wants couples to get married. Relatives nag,

"So, when are you two gonna tie the knot?" To which I used to reply, "As soon as I can get the gag in your mouth." The government wants us married and even bribes us with tax breaks. They'll give us even bigger breaks if we have kids. What is the reason? To make us interdependent, no? So we are raised in a society that coaxes us into interdependence, we become interdependent, and we proceed with our lives. And eventually, unless we die simultaneously or break up, one of us will lose the other. Because of our well-nurtured interdependence, this will likely be the most difficult loss of our lives. If this horrific loss should take place while we are of a proper age for midlife transition, the odds of the event sending us spiraling into a supersonic midlife crisis are very good.

Loss takes many forms and can be the crux of numerous variations on midlife crisis. The comfort zones of our lives are generally built on normality: all that stuff in our immediate periphery that we rely on just to be there for us. This includes our home, our family, our jobs, etc. We may not even like some of these things, but having them where we expect them to be, even if part of us would prefer they weren't, is comforting. So when one or more of those things are taken away, our world gets rocked.

One scenario that is all but universal is known as "Empty Nest Syndrome." This occurs when the kids grow up and leave home. You may not feel it at first, what with all the drinking and naked breakfast-eating, but eventually reality sinks in. A family dynamic is a sensitive thing. It's not just about who needs to get the hell out of the bathroom *now*, it's about the dance of life, the choreography and balance that guides us past one another in hallways and listens for late-night arrivals in our sleep. Our schedules, our societal position, our self-image and our sense of personal responsibility are all heavily influenced by the human contents of our home. When that last kid moves out, the noise may subside but the silence can be deafening.

The intensity of an empty nest loss can be deceiving. Everybody rushes to our aid if someone we love passes (assuming we have people around to do the rushing), but the kids moving out is one that you're just supposed to grin and bear. Perhaps it's the trigger that sets off the MIDMAN's mortality alarms, but it could be the gateway to even more personal discord. Maybe the kids were the glue holding the marriage together. Maybe being alone with a mate for the first time in 20 years illuminates a distance that has grown. Or maybe it's just one more place the MIDMAN is no longer of use. "Father" can be a proud, fun and noble title and wearing a title can support a pretty hearty self-image. Losing a title is a tremendous blow to our self-image whether it's "World Heavyweight Champion" or "Dad." (Fun fact; defending the "Dad" title leaves more facial scars.)

For the MIDMAN between 40 and 62 years of age, the loss of a parent is also pretty common. People usually know their parents their whole lives. Friends may come and go, but parents (or one parent, or step-parents, or parental figures) are always there. Of course this is not true for everyone, but it is for many. So when we lose a parent our entire equilibrium is thrown off. Having a parent is a given, a birthright, so to lose one is like walking outside one night and finding that the moon has left to circle another planet. The moon being gone doesn't necessarily affect our daily life (I know, I know, the tides. Fuck you, I'm taking license) but not having it there creates a persistent void. Yet there's an even more damaging result of losing a parent than simply losing someone important to us.

When we lose a parent we, either consciously or subconsciously, see this event as a confirmation of our own mortality. We tend to view our parents as being as immortal as we view ourselves. Just as we couldn't conceive of our own death before our shitpiphany, our parents' death is out of the question. Our parents are also commonly seen as our protectors. These are often the people we call first when we get good news or bad news. When we lose them we become instantly vulnerable, no matter how old we are when it happens. My favorite line in the film *Mr. Saturday Night* comes up when two brothers, both over 65, who had lost their father years before finally lose their mother and one of them says, "That's it; we're orphans."

We also find that our list of *people we knew who are now passed* is getting a little too long. Once you've got a baker's dozen you can name, you've likely been pushed right over the edge into comprehending your own mortality. Next stop: midlife crisis.

4. Major Loss (professional). Eating regularly and living indoors are items 1 and 2 on my personal priority list. Maintaining these priorities will require making various ongoing payments, which some call 'bills,' to several business entities. Making those payments requires resources, like what some call 'money.' An extended period without resources coming in will eventually discontinue the flow of those resources going out, leaving me in trouble, or what some call 'fucked.' This is why most people have jobs: to support their priorities. But if they lose that job and are faced with the fact that priorities 1 and 2 may not be supported much longer, they are in for a hard time. Surviving on credit cards is never a good option but the average credit card debt (per household with credit card debt) is about $16K, so apparently people are using it as one.

For young people, being out of work is tough enough, but at least they might have the folks to go home to, or a friend they can crash with until they get another job. But for the MIDMAN the situation is much more serious. The young person generally only has himself to fend for but the MIDMAN often covers, or at least shares in, paying the bills that sustain his immediate family, aging parents, the young person mentioned above, home mortgage or rent, car payment, and all the other miscellaneous bills. He probably has no friends to crash with for any serious amount of time, especially if he has family members in tow.

Worse, the job climate for MIDMEN is bleak. The Wall Street Journal published an article stating that "More than 3.5 million Americans between the ages of 45 and 64 were unemployed as of May 2012, 39% of them for a year or more—a rate of long-term unemployment that is unprecedented in modern U.S. history, and far higher than among younger workers. Millions more have quit looking for work." Even those with jobs aren't happy about it. Most people, 80% according to a Deloitte's Shift Index Survey, are dissatisfied with their jobs. If a MIDMAN, who is already likely to be entertaining thoughts of finality and life's brief duration, suddenly gets shit-canned he is ripe for midlife crisis. But the reason for *that* crisis extends well beyond the factors covered so far.

MIDMEN and most other working people attain a lot of their self-esteem from their professions. When we meet new people, "What do you do for a living?" is a question that tends to come up very early in the conversation. "How's business" is as polite and expected a query as "How are you?" and generally people are happy and proud to answer. "Where's the money you owe me, asshole?" is also a very common, financed-based question. What we do for a living is a barometer of how we are progressing through life. The positions and accomplishments themselves provide different indications of status and causes for pride. "My son has a PhD," is a common boast, while "My son has a GED" has never actually been uttered, at least not by my folks. When a MIDMAN loses his job, he also, to a great extent, loses his identity. "I am a ________________," is a statement we want to make with pride. It tells the world that we have value, that we have a place in society. The loss of a job is, in a very real sense, a loss of self. Without the strength of self to gird us against the worst effects of our own aging, we are easily consumed by midlife crisis.

Another way our profession or current job can bring on midlife crisis is by sucking really bad. While being out of work is arguably worse because you can't provide priorities 1 and 2 to yourself, having a shitty job can feel just as bad. It's not so much the day-to-day misery that triggers the crisis, it's the torture of feeling that *this is it*, this is what I have come to. Beyond a sense of victimization there is the feeling of shame. The more his gig runs against the MIDMAN's principals or personal preferences, the deeper the shame.

Yet another cutting of the self-pride tether in middle age is the distance we've moved from our greatest accomplishments. Remember the Springsteen song, *Glory Days*? You should, it was likely a hit while you were enjoying yours! Whether you were a drama club superstar or an athletic miracle, you're likely neither now. In 1987 I spent a few weeks as a reigning Star Search champ and was actually marginally famous. Now I'm just marginal. Adjusting to the post peak *us* is as good a reason as we need to have our midlife crisis.

5. Dissolution of a Primary Relationship. We cannot dismiss the fact that some marriages are destined to fail no matter how patient or dedicated either member of the relationship may be. People change, they grow apart; the magic light of romance is blown out. For the already put-upon MIDMAN this is just another turd in the ol' Dutch oven.

In many relationship-ending midlife crises the snuffing of the 'magical light of romance,' or whatever flowery bullshit I just wrote, may appear to be the cause, but it isn't. It's just another symptom. When the ten-ton weight of impending doom is speeding toward a husband, his fight-or-flight mechanism can kick in. "What can I do to restore my perceived immortality?" he wonders in terms that sound more like, "WHAT THE FUCK!!!???" His tethers to his family and his other responsibilities tighten on him until he can barely breathe. Escape is the only solution he can conjure. He wants to return to the good old days when getting fired from a job didn't portend homelessness, and breaking up with someone didn't require a lawyer. The big problem; even if he escapes from the physical bonds of his job and familial responsibilities, death's intrepid march continues, unimpeded. So, in the hopes that radical change will help slow the clock or at least set it back a few years, these MIDMEN attempt to distance themselves from the external trappings of maturity and aging by breaking ties. The good news is that this strategy can sometimes work. The bad news; the fix is temporary.

So those would be our top five reasons for a midlife crisis. In rare cases a MIDMAN will have a *pure* midlife crisis, one with no easily identifiable trigger. This is the guy who has everything going for him: looks, friends, great family, great job, etc. but suddenly has what I call a pure shitpiphany. So, what does a pure shitpiphany-driven midlife crisis look like? Let me tell you a little story.

I have a friend, I'll call him Hank but he won't answer me because that's not his real name. Hank was 51 but looking not a moment over 45 when his midlife crisis number came up. Hank is a handsome man. He's beefy and rugged in a Nordic kind of way. With his white, toothy smile, his boyish charm and 'I just finished working a hard day and loving it, that's right, *loving* it!' attitude, he is well received by women. Not like that. Hank is married with three kids. The whole family is personable, ambitious and successful. It's actually kind of annoying. Hank was wandering through his life happily, busily and handsomely. He received prolonged looks and inadvertent smiles from women of all ages and returned them with a proper, distant acknowledgment.

One day Hank was buying some do-it-yourselfy thingamabob at a big box home improvement store and found himself on the receiving end of yet another womanly eye lock. This time it was a woman in her late 20s or early 30s. She was a perfectly lovely young woman with whom a man of 45 could actually be seen without raising the ire of our 'it takes a village' society. As usual, Hank tossed her his patented head nod and smile combo that asked *How're ya doin?* but sought no answer. But she didn't perform her part of the scene and stop looking. She actually looked at him more keenly, her eyes narrowing and her smile twisting into a question. *Okay,* Hank thought, *here we go.* This was no ego boost for Hank. He was less a product of his male magnetism than a custodian of it. He understood his effect on women dispassionately and worked his handsomeness like the guy who drives the Caterpillar Earthmover: an expert on operating the machine, but not the machine itself.

Hank saw the confusion in the woman's eyes and her body English suggested that she would soon be walking his way. He assumed that the perplexed look was created for his benefit, and that whatever question she invariably asked would be no more than a pretext for ice breaking. Bingo. With great caution and puzzlement, she stepped his way. Just to be polite, Hank curled his eyes into the classic 'do I know you?' position.

"Mr. Gains?" she asked, the question posed carefully, as if the recipient may have lost his mind or been suffering from amnesia. "It's Carol. Carol Saye? Your daughter Emily's roommate?"

Hank's brain emptied. It had just received information that needed immediate deciphering, and that called for clarity. He thought, this woman is about 30. She has been staring at me and that seemed perfectly normal. She has mistaken me for someone else. And that someone else is the father of her roommate. Who is probably also around 30.

In a matter of 17 syllables, Hank had gone from the object of 30-year-old desire to the father of a 30-year-old. The Pompeii of his reality tumbled around him, pillars falling, crowds running, fires raging, and dogs petrifying. He was a half-beaten boxer staggering toward the wrong corner, a pot of oatmeal over-boiling its starchy froth onto the stovetop.

"I'm sorry," he said when the lights in his head flickered back on, "I'm not Mr. Gains."

"Oh, I am so sorry, sir, I totally thought you were Emily's dad! You look exactly like him! And I was weirded out because I've known Emily's dad, Mr. Gains, my whole life. I'm so glad you're not him or it would have meant he went crazy!" She laughed the laugh of a woman who was not trying to ingratiate herself. No flick of the hair, no theatrical display of coy decorum. She was not treating him like a handsome man; she was treating him like her friend's dad. The boat of his brain rocked in the wake of her indifference. She was—

SIR! Did she just call him sir?! Oh man, this was even worse than he thought.

Hank didn't remember driving home or the perfunctory communication he shared with his family on his way to use the do-it-yourself part he'd just purchased. His mind was like the tumble cycle of a front-loading washing machine, turning his exchange with Emily's roommate over and over and over until it whipped itself into the spin cycle, but from every angle it still brought the worst news he'd ever received; the bell just tolled for he. For the first time Hank found he was undergoing the harshest kind of self-scrutiny. How had he even maintained his illusion of timelessness for so long? Could he survive this instant generational sexual viability shift? Indeed, wouldn't this just be the first of many milestones? Didn't this unfortunate incident essentially confirm that at some point, should the fates not end his life sooner, he would be too old to be attractive to women who were his *current* age?

Or older than his current age!? Or, if time marched on unabated, would his physical form not be rendered totally unattractive, save his value to the owners of various physical therapy clinics and phlebotomy labs? His life had not changed one iota, but his mind would never be the same.

I think it's fair to say that Hank is in the minority in terms of his crisis catalyst. Most men will have definitive circumstance that supports their natural angst. I have outlined the reasons above because you are unlikely to solve a problem as complex as your midlife crisis until you have first identified it—or as legendary American humorist H.L. Mencken said, "There is always an easy solution to every human problem - neat, plausible, and wrong." We have to get a clear-eyed view of our situation before we can hope to conquer it.

Now that we have enjoyed (endured?) an overview of the likely reasons for your condition, let's narrow it down even further. To help accurately identify your personal midlife crisis, I have provided a short quiz. To take this quiz, simply go down the list of questions and choose A or B for each item. You can select both or neither when appropriate. There obviously isn't a time limit, so feel free to actually consider your answers for a moment or two.

	A	B
When I relax I feel	Relaxed	Unproductive
Looking at my body in the mirror makes me feel	Good	Nauseous
I consider myself	Attractive	Not so much
My accomplishments in life make me feel	Successful	Nauseous
My personal relationships are	Rich and rewarding	Financially draining
My career has been	Enriching in many ways	What is this "career" you speak of Earth man?
I can tell I am getting older by the way I	Look	Feel
I carry chewable Pepto-Bismol tablets because I am	Prepared	Nauseous
My health is	Excellent	Behind me
Having a relationship is	Hard work	Someone else's problem
The loss of a loved one(s) has left me feeling	Filthy rich	Sad and vulnerable
When I am out I feel that people	Are aware of me	Don't even see me
Regrets, I've had a few, but then again, too	Few to mention	Many to count
Empty nest syndrome is	Permission to pee with the bathroom door open	A difficult period of loneliness
My finances have left me	A secure future	Yes
All of my life's ambitions have been	Realized	Out of reach
My relationships with others leave me feeling	Socially active	Lonely
(To be read in reggae beat) Don't you worry about a 'ting, 'cause...	Every little 'ting gonna be alright	Some little 'ting gonna end my life
I have been faithful to my significant other	Without fail	Not!
My significant other has been faithful to me	And I appreciate it	Or so they claim...
I am a sexual	Dynamo	Bean bag chair
The state of my health would best be compared to	A man half my age	A medical school cadaver
I want to die	Old and surrounded by loved ones	Please
These questions have made me feel	Enlightened	Nauseous
TOTAL		

As you probably surmised, this is not a pass/fail test. These questions were provided for the simple purpose of putting your feelings in front of you. You'll be reviewing your answers a couple of times as we move forward, but one thing you can note right now is your sense of general well-being. In each question the A answer is positive and the B answer is negative. So if you answered with more Bs than As, it would serve as evidence that you're going through a tougher time.

Many MIDMEN grew up on the cusp of the self-realization epoch and still have trouble admitting that they're going through a tough time. But now we live in an era more accepting of vulnerability. Things have changed radically. In our day, emotional outbursts were reserved for sporting events and drunken best man toasts. Guys these days are actually assumed to have feelings and aren't judged for using prescribed anti-anxiety meds. Never mind 'aren't judged,' some MIDMEN get so twisted they can get their drugs bought for them like a round of drinks! "Hey Steve, you've turned into a real asshole. How about a nice, icy cold Xanax on me?"

Adjusting to this sensitive new world is tough for a lot of us. Let's be honest here, your garden variety MIDMAN hasn't spent much time down at 'Huggy Dave's Touchy Feely Gym and Spa' working out his poor-wittle-me muscles. We're not big on looking inward. Answering certain questions in the quiz above was probably shitty for you, but I promise it's tough love. Now go back and look at the answers again, bitch. Sorry, I got carried away. Seriously, take all the time you need to examine them. If you didn't actually mark the page that's okay, you're going to come up with the same answers. We'll meet back here.

Seeing a list of your feelings on these issues and considering how they impact you directly exposes a combination of key elements that make your midlife crisis unique. If you're suffering because of a reason or reasons identified above, that's good; now you can address it. However, while each item is a justifiable reason for your mental state, they are not all equal. For instance, the anxiety generated by being deep in debt could easily trump the peace of mind provided by a faithful spouse. Living with all of the psychological elements of midlife crisis—which occurs even under alleged *perfect life* circumstances and then adding a bonus layer of debt or empty nest or ill health can be too much. Identifying a specific soul-sapper like deep debt and holding it away from the other negative B answers in the quiz automatically fixes your focus on it, brings it out into broad daylight. So what do you do? What *do* you do?

The "good" news about problems like debt or being overweight is that generally there are solutions. The solutions aren't always easy, but they can be approached and we will do just that in subsequent chapters. In almost every situation where a proactive approach to problem solving is required, the key factor for success is honesty. We have to assess the situation honestly, approach other parties like bankers or family honestly, and act with continued honesty. This is of course ironic, since our midlife crisis is in no small way the result of our having been involuntarily honest with ourselves! We MIDMEN frequently beat ourselves up about what losers we are, how weak we've become, how we've fucked up the opportunities life has handed us over the years, etc. Occasionally, we're correct in our self-debasement so honesty is, frankly, not our friend! There's an old English proverb that says, "A man is not old until his regrets take the place of his dreams." The MIDMAN stands at that crucial crossroad where he can still make a strong move toward achieving the dreams he was unable to fulfill as a younger man, but can also see permanent regrets taking form.

Now go through the quiz one *more* time and check your spelling. Just kidding. Go through the test again, but this time when you've answered a question with a B choice, ask yourself if the situation is changeable or not. For example, someone dying is not changeable but loneliness is. I'll check my email while I wait for you.

Okay, did you see that virtually *all* of the situations could be changed in some way? Of course there are some deeply personal or individual problems that require an individualized solution, like coping with big legal or physical problems, but some problems are much more common than others. Some extend into so many areas that solving one will solve many.

In the following chapters I will be breaking down the problems listed above and outlining some methods for marginalizing them. The goal here is to isolate the primary non-midlife crisis problems in our lives and dispatch them via one method or another so that we can go after the Big Kahuna: our actual midlife crisis. Remember, the philosophy of this book is:

1. I'm actually getting old.
2. It's ultimately going to suck.
3. Tough shit. I will still need to live life to the fullest until I can't anymore.

We cannot attempt to live life to the fullest in the middle of all the distracting bullshit life visits upon us unless we have a very clear understanding of what matters to us. And we cannot clearly identify what matters to us until we eliminate a whole bunch of distracting bullshit along the way. It's a nasty cycle. So, in the chicken or the egg-like riddle of pursuing what matters or overcoming that which blocks us from pursuing what matters, we will have to choose one to come first.

Virtually every problem you revealed by taking the quiz above is just a roadblock. Granted, some are far more substantial and life-altering than others, but they all stand between you and the real answer to the question "What truly matters?" A MIDMAN lying on his deathbed who has lived his life pursuing what matters to him will have lived well. He won't even have to complete anything successfully. He could conceivably fuck up everything he touches. But if he lives his life in pursuit of the thing or things that matter to him, it will be the *pursuit* and not the *result* that will fill his minutes, days and years. Never forget this;

it takes a long time to reach a worthy goal but only seconds to utter the words "I'm done." This means you fucking well better enjoy the process of reaching that goal because *that* is how you spend your life.

Below you will find another quizzy thing. It lists some common goals that we MIDMEN have. All you have to do is rate your desire to achieve each one on a four-point scale. One means you *don't* really give shit about it, and four means you *do* really give a shit about it. This time actually use a writing instrument, as you'll want to be able to review the answers easily after you're done. A Ticonderoga Number 2 pencil would be customary, or so the GED test proctor told me.

	RATING			
DESIRES	**DON'T give a shift**			**DO give a shift**
1. Get in shape	1	2	3	4
2. Travel	1	2	3	4
3. Rise to a challenge (climb Everest, build a brick barbeque, run for office, etc.)	1	2	3	4
4. Pursue creative outlet (sing, dance, do standup, write a book, record music, publish photography, etc.)	1	2	3	4
5. Start your own business (patent your invention, open a restaurant, etc.)	1	2	3	4
6. Expand your social circle (find a new relationship, buddies, etc.)	1	2	3	4
7. Pick up and move your life (new home, new state, new country, etc.)	1	2	3	4
8. Learn a new skill (language, musical instrument, etc.)	1	2	3	4
*	1	2	3	4

* If your personal desire was not on the list you are a freak and I'm going to have to ask you to get out of my book. Or you can write it in and rate it, though I assume the rating will be four.

While many MIDMEN are able to maintain some enthusiasm for their ambition(s), most have let them drift away like Leonardo DiCaprio's chilly little hands in *Titanic*. The point of this exercise is not only to put your dreams or ambitions in front of you, but also to have you determine your priorities. If, say, my neighbor's dog is continuing its five-year yapping marathon while I'm taking the quiz and I'm thinking, "Yeah, I'd like to pack up and move!" it may not be a number 4 priority. Maybe it's a 2. But if I've been feeling really guilty about not taking my clarinet out of the attic *and* I've been spending serious time in the mirror hating on my fat gut, I have a genuine pair of 4s (bonus blackjack tip: split the 4s vs. 5/6 if you can double after the split. Only double 4s vs 7 or less in a single deck game where the dealer is staying on 17.)

Some items listed in the quiz may require other items to be accomplished before they can even be considered. Sure, the morbidly obese can start a business or clean and jerk a harmonica to their mouths, but that week on the Appalachian Trail is going to put you in a world of hurt. If you're not already in good shape physically, item #1 is already your highest priority. Your health is your number one concern, so if you didn't do this, go circle 4 on the first item. I'll be kicking this dead horse (though, being pescatarian I won't be eating it) over and over as we go along, but basically the point is if you get sick, or especially if you die, you are of no use to yourself or anyone else. I have a dear friend I love like a brother who's carrying around a lot of extra weight (actually I have about six friends who fit that description. I'm just hoping they each think it's them I'm referring to). He has bills and kids (oops, narrowed it to four) and he could drop dead at any second, anywhere. I've already had about six friends do exactly that. It's horrible for the people around them. People lose best friends, kids lose dads, families lose homes, and wives marry secret boyfriends. Literally, as I write this chapter, a friend announced on Facebook that a guy he had been on the phone with just a few hours earlier was now dead of a heart attack. I checked his page; he was much too heavy. If you're an unhealthy fat guy nobody wants to tell you you're actually under the imminent threat of sudden death, so here are three great reasons for you to switch to a nice salad and a glass of water instead of Mickey Ds:

- Jerry Garcia, dead at 53. Did he do heroin? Yeah, but that's not what killed him. William Burroughs lived to 83 and abused heroin right to the end. Jerry got himself up as high as 300 pounds, was diabetic, and smoked like a chimney. Heart stopped.
- John Candy, dead at 43. Three hundred pounds of funny on a 6-foot-2-inch frame. You're a MIDMAN so I know you loved him. His family had a history of heart problems, but that didn't stop him from packing on the pounds and smoking heavily. He left behind his wife Rosemary, his two children, Jennifer and Christopher, and all the rest of us.
- And of course, James Gandolfini, dead at 51. Okay, so how tough are you? Tougher than Tony fucking Soprano?! I do not think so. He won a Golden Globe, Screen Actors Guild Award, three Emmys, and then the coveted Heart Attack Award.

Do you want people as pissed off at you for dying unnecessarily as you are at the guys listed above? Don't you owe *somebody* the respect of remaining alive? I'll get into actual ways to get healthier later in the chapter THE BODY but for now, allow me to speak on behalf of the friends and relations of MIDMEN who are taunting death with their weight and lifestyle: *Get serious about working this shit out, you selfish fuck*!!!

Another roadblock to approaching the quiz items that you rated 3 or 4 could be depression. When you're totally bummed you really don't want to do shit. Depression is a bitch and being a MIDMAN—you remember, we're the guys with the highest suicide rates?—the odds of you having a bit of it are very good. My mother the shrink and an objective third-party shrink agree that I have a manic personality. I have been "self-medicating" with, um, I want to say holistic? treatments since I was a kid. During my midlife crisis proper I also allowed myself to be professionally medicated with actual prescribed anti-anxiety stuff. I understand what it's like to wake up and not want get out of bed . . . ever again. It may have been that I viewed myself as such a wretched loser that even trying anything would be an act of futility, or it may have been that I was experiencing actual physical pain. But I dared to look honestly at the 4s on my list, and there were a few for me, and I refused to let them slip away. I am not presumptuous enough to assume that I can throw down a paragraph or two and rid you of crippling depression. But I will say this; to cure depression, you need to put whatever energy you can muster behind the accomplishment of a single goal: curing your depression. It's a balancing act; your priorities have to compete directly with your depression-fueled inaction. There are many ways to combat depression and other mental roadblocks like OCD but the most important thing is to man up and admit the problem exists. You're not fooling anyone anyway so you might as well work it out. Talk to a friend, talk to your wife, talk to your smartest kid, go on a diet, take a walk, see a shrink, try a med; live!

Okay, so assuming you have the physical ability and cheery disposition to carry on, let's have another look at the quiz. One of those 4s (or 3s if no 4s) should kind of stand out to you. One way to ascertain this is by considering how willing you are to make sacrifices for it. *Desire* choices like bedding younger women or owning a Lamborghini have been purposely omitted. For one thing, no shit. But more importantly, the MIDMAN's troubled soul will not be mollified by those things. They might make for one hell of a weekend, but they won't solve the bigger problems of self-worth or mortality in the long run.

Once you have narrowed your choices to your key goal, consider why you aren't in heated pursuit of it. A pang of guilt indicates that you haven't fulfilled some promise to yourself. As we take our high speed trip on the Midlife Transition Express (All aboard! Next stop, *Oldfucksville*!), we need to get off at various stops along the way to follow our dreams.

The trick to happy aging and, ultimately, guiltless death, is not necessarily having accomplished our goals; it is having spent our lives in pursuit of them. As a man who has spent much of his life pursuing happily and succeeding infrequently, I know this to be true from personal experience. As I wrote above, it takes months or years to reach a goal and only seconds to say the words, "I'm done." There is little *other* than the pursuit, so you *must* learn to dig on it.

Pursuing our passion also offers us distraction. At a time of life when our minds involuntarily surrender themselves to obsessing over who we have become, how fast time is passing and what we're going to do about it, some distraction is just what the doctor ordered. This, unfortunately, is where the girls and the Lamborghinis come in. We are so desperate to redefine our self-image that we go for the lowest hanging fruit. Instead of "I am a divorced father of two with a livable job that doesn't challenge me anymore," we get to see ourselves as some kind of James Bond. But we're not really James Bond and playing dress-up for a while won't address our larger self-esteem and quality of life issues. No less than movie star Hugh Grant—he of the British accent, supermodel ex-wife, and hooker scandal—admitted that at 51 he was having a genuine midlife crisis. Apparently you can't car, cash or girl your way out of it, so you are reduced to finding meaning. Sorry.

The greatest barrier separating our realistic, personally gratifying solution from a superficial, ego candy band-aid solution is the world in which we live. You can't really move through society to pursue the goals that actually matter to you without the media pushing cars and girls at you. Worse still, the ad agencies are using your already embarrassingly weak defenses against you in careful, scientifically proven ways. You are essentially being hypnotized into thinking that what you want is cars and girls. Advertisers are very clever because they are trying to sell you something you already want, or use something you already want to sell you everything else. The Carl's Jr. commercial featuring Paris Hilton in a bikini washing a Bentley is a perfect example. You're already genetically predisposed to want the girl (assuming you are genetically predisposed to wanting girls), you have societal conditioning to want the car and *then* they throw in the burger. But the truth is that none of the elements of that commercial would provide you with any kind of foundation for lasting happiness, though selling the Bentley and marrying the Hilton could keep you living indoors and eating burgers for quite a while (seriously though, don't eat the burgers).

Okay, so why aren't you spending the bulk of your limited years basking in the sheer joy of pursuing your dreams? Probably because you have been alive for about half a century, give or take, and you have placed yourself in a situation that is not conducive to the quest. Unfortunately, you are unlikely to die for several more years. This means you're going to have to either live with the self-loathing generated by your continued screwing of yourself out of the things you truly want, or you're going to have to step up. The thing to remember here is that you don't just *want* to pursue your goals; you *need* to pursue them.

Any time you spend in pursuit of what matters to you is time well-spent. Avoiding your goals takes exactly the same amount of time as working to accomplish them, so that shouldn't be a factor. But there are legitimate reasons why pursuing our goals could be challenging. Now that you have established your *desires* based on the survey earlier, take your highest priority and, assuming you are not currently working toward it, use the survey below to determine why not.

	SEVERITY			
CHALLENGES	**Not at all**			**Extremely**
1. History (bad credit, sullied reputation, legal troubles)	1	2	3	4
2. Personal obligations (familial, financial, etc.)	1	2	3	4
3. Lack of information (no expertise in area of interest, etc.)	1	2	3	4
4. Location (ambition not geographically feasible or lack of personal space, etc.)	1	2	3	4
5. Physical (ill health, incapacitated, etc.)	1	2	3	4
6. Time (current responsibilities trump ambitions, etc.)	1	2	3	4
7. Financial (debts, obligations, work hours, etc.)	1	2	3	4
8. Support (emotional)	1	2	3	4
*	1	2	3	4

* Again, you may have a formidable challenge that doesn't fit one of the categories listed. If that's the case, just add it on in there and give it a four.

The challenges above are not negligible and I hope that by naming them I don't appear to be diminishing their influence. In fact, some combinations create conditions that make pursuing a goal all but impossible. Others might be simple but summoning the energy and initiative is tough. To meet this book's goal of lifting the MIDMAN reader out of midlife crisis, he has to accomplish two primary things:

1. Isolate and identify the pursuit or pursuits in his life that will offer enhanced value to his blink-of-the-eye visit to planet Earth.
2. Clear a pathway through the everyday shit that comprises his current life so he can pursue the pursuit(s) he's identified as the pursuit(s) he wishes to pursue.

While we are permanently enclosed within our bodies, regardless of health, and led by our brains, regardless of mental state, our physical surroundings are the next most influential factor in our ability to derive the personal satisfaction that smites midlife crisis. Let's move on to the next chapter and figure out how to negotiate our immediate environment in a progressive way, shall we? After you (age before beauty).

Chapter 3

THE RADIUS

"A successful man is one who can lay a firm foundation with the bricks others have thrown at him."

David Brinkley

What is your radius? You are the center of your universe in that everything extends infinitely in every direction from exactly where you are now reading. Fortunately, some things are so far from the "you" center of the universe that they don't require your ongoing consideration – things like planets, stars and Inuit peoples. But the things close to you directly affect what I am hereby declaring your 'radius.' These include every single living or inanimate thing you observe or experience directly in any way, whether it's the sound of a distant dog barking or the smell of your Indian neighbors cooking the shit out of something completely gross but somehow stomach growl-inducing, it's your radius.

Like an air traffic controller, we sit in the tower of our minds and try to effectively orchestrate the incoming and outgoing *flights* or events that enter our radius. A communication from the tower might go something like this:

You, the Central Control Tower

Teen P.U.B. 15, I cannot clear you for departure for soccer practice delivery. You're third in line for takeoff behind Dog Pissed R.U.G. #1 and B.O.S.S. Call #2. Do you copy?

Teen P.U.B. 15

Yeah, roger that Tower, I copy. Code W.T.F, dude? This sucks. I hate you.

You, the Central Control Tower

Copy that. Teen P.U.B. 15, you are grounded.

The idea that all the elements of our lives can be effortlessly organized in a way that prevents crashes is absurd. So, like an air traffic controller, we have to be vigilant and study the radar screen that is the periphery of our existence and maneuver the elements in ways that make our day-to-day reality most tolerable.

Not everyone can immediately identify the primary disturbances within their radius. This is because some obvious things may not be as distracting as some less noticeable things. The radius is a delicate and persnickety thing and controlling it requires that we first understand what it is exactly that is disturbing it.

The test below is designed to help you sort through the cacophony of your radius and highlight the areas that most need controlling so you can identify and indulge what truly matters to you. Answer the questions below and be honest with yourself here because it could really help you identify the areas of your radius that most need control. No matter what your personal circumstances, what you do for a living, how many people you may live with or your financial means, all the questions should apply to you.

	Always	Sometimes	Never

1. Life in my house is:

a. Medieval torture
b. Just fucking great, *okay?!*
c. Manageable
d. Pretty okay
e. Kind of cool
f. Bliss

2. Overall, I think people are:

a. Shitty
b. Uncool
c. Tolerable
d. Pretty okay
e. Mostly cool
f. Great

	Always	Sometimes	Never
3. I am responsible for deciding when I:			
a. Work			
b. Eat			
c. Read			
d. Sleep			
e. Watch TV, see sports, movies, etc.			
f. Have sex			
4. I wish the following circumstances were different for me:			
a. Job/career			
b. Marriage			
c. Family (kids, siblings, parents)			
d. Home			
e. Physical appearance			
f. Health			
g. Sex life			
5. I believe my problems could be solved if I had more:			
a. Money			
b. Time			
c. Hair			
d. Dick			
e. Friends			
f. Ambition			

While this quiz was constructed to be informative, it also serves as a fun drinking game! Just look through your answers and every time you see an answer that makes you feel particularly pathetic, take a drink.

Your answers to this test have just exposed many of the darkest, most hidden truths of your life. Actually, this test is so revealing I've changed my mind; don't put your answers in the book. If someone finds it you'll be ruined. Instead create a side sheet with the answers that can correlate with the questions. What? Too late? Already marked it up? Okay then, hide or destroy these pages the second we're done here. Maybe you should eat them. I'm sorry, you know what? You're far too exposed now and I'm going to have to disavow any knowledge of you. Your MIDMEN reading mission is terminated and you are dead to me.

Our radius is not only formed or influenced by *others*, our own personal shit is a huge factor. By using the term "shit" I don't mean to refer only to the things that are commonly referred to as "shit," like weed or the stuff you left at an ex-girlfriend's house (as in, "Come get your shit or I'm throwing it on the fucking lawn, asshole!"). I'm also not referring to the sharing of your actual doody. That is something one is rarely put upon to share. Not never necessarily, just rarely. Actually, I recently had a doctor request some of my doody and even though I was being asked to share something beyond worthless, I still somehow felt kind of stingy.

Your shit is actually far less your personal possessions than it is your emotional and intellectual shit. Our shit and the way it's meted out has a direct or indirect impact not only on our personal selves, but also on everyone around us. So we have to constantly make judgments regarding how we choose to deal with the shit of others and conversely, how we direct the trajectory and strength of our shit. This "balancing of shit" (which was also the name of the worst Cirque Du Soleil act I ever saw) is at the core of our surviving happily. How we go about doing this is what I call "Controlling Your Radius."

By way of example let us assume for a moment that you are kind of a dick. What? I'm just saying *as an example*. Okay, so you're a total dick. And maybe you have perfectly valid reasons for being a dick. Maybe your life too often places you in the eye of a frustrating radius hurricane. So you, in all your justified dickiness, make your dissatisfaction known to the world with an outward projection of dickatude. Seems like a perfectly fair exchange; you're frustrating me with your stupid bullshit and I am communicating my disapproval plainly in the lingua franca of dicks, *Dicklish*. There are two problems with this particular action and reaction: one, everyone thinks you're a dick because you're being a dick, and two, you're the one who has to *be* a dick, which is never a good time. You're forced to try and negotiate your life through terrible external *and* internal disruptions in your radius, one caused by the forces that be and the other created by you. Buddha himself said, "You will not be punished for your anger, you will be punished *by* your anger," so put that in your dick and smoke it.

Some believe we can manage our radius through an ancient Hindu concept called "karma." It means, basically, we get back what we put out and it allegedly works like this; the airline check-in person upgrades me to business class because I helped an old woman push her old husband into the airport, assuming of course he was in a wheelchair. In essence, I am expected to go out and perform life's little niceties, like holding doors for people, in the hopes that other niceties will fly home on the wings of my well-earned good fortune. I don't buy the ethereal universal balance theory, but if we observe the notion of karma in a very pragmatic, terrestrial way we start to see something logical. Here's a really easy, basic example that comes up all the time. I will hold a door for some fucking dolt who will walk through, brain dead, without so much as a thank you glance. Okay, so now I have a choice. I can resent myself for having extended this courtesy to someone so undeserving, or I can accept that what I am doing is making sure that I live in a world where somebody holds the fucking door for somebody by actually being the somebody who holds it. As famous father of the Indian independence movement and diaper model, Mahatma Gandhi, once said, "Be the change that you want to see in the world." Not surprisingly, his diaper was changed immediately. Too soon?

Now if we expand on that concept and apply it to just about every interaction we encounter in our lives, we may actually improve our lot in life. We are at least 50% of every personal interaction in our radius; how we choose to accept and respond to those interactions isn't just a method of coping, it quite literally dictates the way we live our minute-by-minute life.

Our radius includes everything and everyone that affects us. Attempting to control such a Radius is pretty challenging but it kind of has to be done. We're trying to create a world where we can maintain access to our happy place until everything goes to shit and then we die (fun fact: accessing our happy place in public can be a misdemeanor).

As you read the following chapters consider how the subject of each factors into your radius control.

Chapter 4

THE SPOUSE

"When a husband brings his wife flowers for no reason,
there's a reason."
Molly McGee (Fibber McGee & Molly)

THE SPOUSE

Pliny the Elder said, "Home is where the heart is." I'm no doctor, but I believe the ole Plinster confused his home with his chest cavity. For most of us, home is different from any other place on Earth. This is where we can look our absolute shittiest, smell our worst, and behave most like the pieces of shit that we are. In our home we are many things but one of them is not "a mystery." As we march on defiantly toward our goal of creating the circumstances for discovering, accessing and implementing the things that matter to us, managing the place we call home is crucial. The first question you answered in that last quiz was "Life in my house is (blank)." There are really two distinct components to that question; one addresses living alone, the other addresses having other living organisms surround us, more often than not including a spouse.

Experts are of two minds on the benefits of group habitation. *The Journal of Epidemiology and Community Health* (and I'm sure like me you can't wait for your copy to show up in the mailbox) finds that people who never married were 58% more likely to die than married people! I will assume they mean die prematurely, as 100% of us are odds-on favorites to die. Meanwhile, they add, widowed people are 40% more mortal. Divorced or separated folks? Twenty-seven percent more likely to die. But there's the other side of the story.

Del Webb is the name of a company that operates 59 so-called "active adult retirement communities" across the USA. By "adult" they mean that at least one member of the household is over 55, which is late for a MIDMAN, but you'll be there before you know it. According to a 2013 Del Webb survey of 521 single boomers ages 50 and older, only 11% of single respondents said they would prefer to be married. That's men *and* women, by the way. The men, by a large majority, named "...having the time and freedom to engage in hobbies and social activities they didn't get to in the past" as the primary reason they liked being single. That said, 56% are fine with dating, which may well be a hobby or social activity they didn't get to in the past.

But single life is not a panacea, nor does not having anyone else around the house to get in our way substantially reduce our need for radius control. If we live alone, we still have to create an environment that is conducive to our happiness, and historically, men who live alone suck at that. Actually, it's not just men. The Finnish Institute of Occupational Health conducted some research from 2000 to 2008 and found that people living alone are more likely to use antidepressants. As I've mentioned, MIDMEN are the demo most committed to committing suicide and MIDMEN living alone, either as a result of divorce, becoming a widower or by personal preference, represent more than 50% of attempted suicides.

Marital problems, unhappy or ended love affairs, or the recent loss of a loved one (particularly among older people) can trigger suicidal depression. Often one factor, like a friendship-ending fight or one of those deadly little surprise parties that sometimes result from our annual physicals, is the last straw in a series of upsetting circumstances. I should mention that the previous facts were brought to you courtesy of Merck Pharmecuticals, makers of Elavil™. Depressed? Middle aged? Pop yourself an Elavil. Elavil can also treat chronic fatigue syndrome, irritable bowel syndrome and bedwetting. Warning: Do not operate machinery while wetting the bed.

If the only other occupants of your living space are the people who inhabit your video games or sex fantasies—or both if you're playing Bonecraft™ (yes, it's a real game. I'll save you the trip; two Elf chicks going at each other's *hröars* while an *Orc* that looks like Ron Jeremy fucks one of them *Wargy*-style)—then your chance of depression is higher.

If you really don't want to live alone and aren't sure how to hook yourself up, the first thing you have to make yourself is proactive. Actually, that may be the second thing. The first might be to turn yourself into better barter. If you want a mate, then you want to be at least the same level of catch as the mate you're hoping to meet. The upcoming THE BODY chapter will give you lots of advice on how to upgrade yourself physically, but once you do, you'll still have to get yourself out there. Here are two smart ways to start meeting the next ex-Mrs. You:

1. Online dating sites. These are the easiest way to meet someone. The best thing about these sites is that you can establish, or eliminate the possibility of a relationship before you even have to shower. Exchanging messages or IMs on a dating site is a great way to break the ice without fear of commitment. It's also efficient. Rather than having to learn about your potential match via conversation, many of the answers will already be written out for you. Beyond easy stuff like age, job and location, questionnaires for the profiles on dating sites like Match.com feature queries like: last book read, marital status (!), any body art, income, etc.

   The sites are, for the most part, intuitive and easy to use, which is nice. Another nice thing about them is your odds; the three biggest sites according to TopTenRatings.com offer a gender ratio very favorable to MIDMEN. Match.com is 43/57 female with 65% of members being over 35 years old; eHarmony.com reports a staggering 29/71 split favoring female members with 64% over 35; and PerfectMatch.com is a little closer at 40/60 female but 70% are over 35. None of the sites are free, but people do meet, sex is had, and relationships sometimes actually do survive.

2. The lowest hanging fruit for single MIDMEN trying to find a match may well also be the sweetest: divorced moms. YourTango.com offered a great argument for MIDMEN to consider single MILFs. I'll paraphrase to condense their findings: 1) They don't want trouble; they've *had* trouble. They just want to enjoy their lives. 2) They're in or around their sexual peak and they are likely to repeatedly blow your . . . mind. 3) They don't want more kids. 4) They've got more balls than younger women who have never been through childbirth and divorce. 5) They want to communicate with you as a grown-up. They have kids to provide all the whining and nagging they need in their lives.

   There are plenty of divorced moms out there on the dating sites and plenty of men who, foolishly, don't want to date them so if you can make yourself desirable, you will be plenty desired!

Like cohabitating, living alone is habit forming. One advantage it offers is the freedom to live the way you want to live. If you don't want to wash the fucking dishes, you don't have to wash the fucking dishes. If you don't want pick up your shit and put it away, you don't have to pick up your shit and put it away. The same with taking out the garbage, doing laundry, bathing, and on and on. However, MIDMEN are at an age where college dorm-style living is more than just immature, it's very telling. It reveals any number of possible personality traits in the liver ("liver" as in one who lives this way, not the organ you're ruining with the shitty beer that used to occupy the empty cans all over your place). For instance, is the mess a means to an end? Do you have other reasons to believe that you may not be good company and would prefer to disabuse yourself of the unfathomable idea of visitors in your home by making your home impossible to invite them to?

Living life to the fullest means doing alive stuff like going places and seeing people. It means making plans and having hopes and chasing dreams and feeling success and failure. Sitting in your underwear on top of some other pair of underwear you're not wearing anymore while watching a game on TV and drinking a shitty beer (seriously, try the Belgian Ales) is not officially "living," it's taking a break from life. If you behave when you're feeling fine the way busy people behave only when they've got the flu, you are doing it wrong. Married men enjoy the benefit of another set of eyes on them to keep them in check. Even guys with roommates have someone who will at some point say, "Dude, I mean, fuck. You know?" But if you live alone your checks and balances are all on you.

Women are naturally predisposed to something called *nesting*. Essentially, nesting just means setting up housekeeping. We assume that evolution shaped women's habits thusly because they are likely to need a proper place to birth their young'uns. Men lack this reptilian instinct. As the hunters in the hunter/gatherer roles that separate the genders, we are predisposed to sleep on dirt and poop in holes. Modern men now living in civilized dwellings should have evolved beyond our primitive inclinations, but no. An uninspired man left alone in the penthouse suite at the Bellagio in Las Vegas long enough will, in one form or another, wind up sleeping on dirt and pooping in a hole. Like the launch pad of a NASA rocket, MIDMEN need a stable platform from which to take off. Self-respect and energy are both integral to item 3 in the MIDMEN process of life meme, "live life to the fullest." It is hard for us to respect ourselves when we know we're not maintaining ourselves well.

Being out of shape physically and living in chaos, confusion or filth act as a severe obstacle to our ability to discover ourselves or pursue the things that really matter to us. This does not only refer to the evolution of career or personal goals; if you would like to be touched by another person for free, or invite anyone who isn't as gross as you into your life, pulling your shit together is essential. Even if you lack a spouse or the impetus to land one, you should at least live as if it might be possible. Keeping your person clean and living in a place sanitary enough for a date to get naked in are good things in general. A spouse will generally help "inspire" us (read: plant a foot in our ass) to keep things thus.

Marital satisfaction is often described as a long-term U-curve, but then so is Peyronie's disease. People generally affirm that their marriages are happiest during the early years and not as happy during the MIDMAN years. Marital satisfaction increases once again in the later years, once finances have stabilized and parenting responsibilities have ended. Couples who stay together until after the last child has left home will probably remain married for at least another 20 years.

If you're a 35-65 year-old man and in a marriage, then the person you are married to has the most impact on your life and vice versa. While you're going through your version of "Oh, fuck, my career" or "Oh, fuck, my dreams" or "Oh, fuck, my genetic predisposition toward prolific promiscuity," you may not be considering the person closest to you in the proper perspective. If you're married to a reasonable peer in terms of age, then you live with someone who is also freaking out. Our own freaking-out can render us oblivious to a lot of the things around us. Most of those things can go fuck themselves, but your partner's circumstances affect your radius so significantly that their mental state is actually a component of yours. We need to curb our crisis to the extent that we can perceive what is happening with the most important person in our life who isn't us—really see that person and empathize with what they're going through in *their* lives, so that we can more easily manipulate them into doing our evil bidding. The problem with this scenario is it requires honesty both inward and outward. But as 19th century French hipster prototype Jean Giraudoux memorably said, "The secret of success is sincerity. Once you can fake that you've got it made."

There are fewer issues of more pressing importance to the married MIDMAN than behavior toward his, assumedly, middle-aged wife. Two middle-aged people coping with their respective gender's midlife shit under the same roof can be a real pressure cooker. When things aren't meshing there's a sort of alchemy at play. It can trigger the creation of a domestic hot zone, a territorial battle of wills replete with volleys of verbal shit missiles flying across the *mine, mine, mine* field.

I know I'm repeating myself a lot, but women are going through an extremely difficult time at exactly the same time we are. Just as we worry about age, the speeding advance of time, and our inevitable deaths, our female counterparts are enduring the same thing but it's actually harder for her, so seriously dude, come on.

Let me illustrate it thusly; in 1987 or so Botox was discovered. In 2011, Botox was injected 5.8 million times (that's just here in the USA) and brought in $1.8 billion. Almost two *BEEELLLLEEEONNN* dollars! I'm guessing none of it was shot into you. Sure, some MIDMEN may manscape meticulously, whiten their teeth or work out purely for appearance (coughing into hand, *"me"*), but these little expressions of vanity are nothing compared to those of most of the ladies. Do any of your guy friends wear Spanx? I thought not.

Nearly two billion dollars' worth of Botox shots. Why do you figure that is? I'll tell you why: men are to a large degree visually attracted. And in this regard we are exceedingly well served. Images of desirable women permeate the landscape wherever the landscape provides a surface to plaster them. The women we see displayed in these venues are more often than not youthful. This is because we are genetically directed to seek out females with which we can create progeny. This doesn't mean we *want* progeny, or will always admit to it when confronted with the news that we have partnered in the creation thereof, but we are programmed to propagate the species. So, to remain attractive to us—and I need to reiterate, this is on a DNA level, not necessarily an intellectual one—women are compelled to try and look younger. Of course the cosmetic and fashion marketers foster these feelings of insecurity about age in our wives.

There has been much written about the invisibility of the middle-aged woman, usually by middle-aged women, which means by her own definition she's invisible, which leads people to wonder, "Who wrote this?" Women spend a good chunk of their lives as the subject of unchecked male lust. If a woman doesn't know that men have been thinking about fucking her throughout a large portion of her life, she just didn't ask . . . or the guys didn't. At a certain point, however, the volume of the attention can wane a bit. So, the woman attempts to restore herself to the version that got the whistles. But it's really not directly about the whistles or the fuck-wanting. It's really about attention. So how do we alleviate our wife's insecurity about her appearance or, more importantly, about the substance of our adoration, so that she can bring her A-game to our self-serving little lives? Simple: consideration.

When we as husbands go above and beyond to be considerate, it is interpreted quite correctly as our noticing our wives or significant others. If your wife is cold and you get her something warm; if she's upset and you actually tune in and listen; if she needs to use the bathroom and you stop prairie dogging it, spray and get the hell out; if you can actually not respond to a criticism or correction defensively, you are paying attention to her. Having a wife who feels she is being acknowledged is ultimately good for your radius control. Let's be clear: when she is sending out the good vibes, you get good vibes. Since you live within those vibes, when *they're* good it's all good. You want your wife, even when she hates the world, giving you the love.

All too often we are the ones who are sullen about the other aspects of our lives that aren't pleasing us (probably because we're not pursuing what matters to us, if I may beat that drum again). We might be under slept or under-fed or we might have a chemical imbalance. Whatever the reason, if we are harshing her lady buzz, she is likely to send the harsh back like a boomerang. If we are totally honest with ourselves and believe we are the initiator of the problem, then we have to cut the shit. Who wins if we don't?

If like me you've tried controlling your committed other by way of raised voice, passive aggression or general shittiness, you know as well as I do that even when it does work, it doesn't work. Sure, it may keep her at a distance for a while, but while I'm sitting there in my hard-fought solitude, I'm all twisted up and pissed off. The battle can't be won that way. She has to give a shit about my getting what I want for me to actually enjoy it when I get it. This means I have to keep her feeling as though I give a shit about her. Of course I do give a shit about her, but not quite as giant a shit as I give about myself. Admit it, you're the same. And it's not just your domestic other; it's everybody. Would you take a bullet for your wife or kids? Sure you would. It would be a reflex. But reflexive acts of true love are different than "generous" acts. Most of us have enough sense to perform some of them. Orgasming last is a good example. Removing dead things or particularly icky live things from places where they aren't wanted is another. Controlling your radius when it comes to your spouse means servicing some select needs so that you are free to pursue your deplorable selfishness. Consider this: do you get any shit for watching a game if there's nothing big being neglected? Less likely, right? So even though surrendering to the lowly labors of household drudgery or honey-do list shit is a concept you reject down into the dark, seething core of your being, not doing it severely undermines your radius control.

Anaïs Nin, the worldly French eroticist and internationally recognized Henry Miller fucker said, "When you make a world tolerable for yourself you make a world tolerable for others." The opposite is even truer. For example, there is a little act of spousal radius control I implemented in my house. In some ways I am a slob. For instance, I like to take off my white ankle cut sweat socks and hang them on my ears. Then I tilt my head and stare at my wife like a confused puppy. It's a thing. When I complete the ritual, I drop the socks wherever I happen to be standing at the moment. Wives stand in united opposition to frivolously discarded socks, and my wife is no exception. However, a few months ago I told my wife that I would be handling the dishes. I don't mind washing dishes and she hates it so it was a nice, painless overture on my part. Let me tell you something, brother; if you're washing all the dishes you can leave your socks wherever the fuck you want! That said, as soon as we struck the deal she raced out and bought a cookbook called *Recipes That Require Every Pot and Pan in the Fucking House*.

Don't think about servicing your needs first; think about how satisfying the needs of *others* can service your needs. Here's a mantra you can earworm into your skull and live by: "Selfish Selflessness."

Even if you are a raging douche, your partner may still actually suck. It reminds me of the old chestnut about the woman enduring that time of the month who screams, "Just because I'm having my period doesn't mean you're not an asshole!" Or you might be a patient, considerate, and decent guy who deserves respect and love and a better writer than me. In either event, if your marital partner is not someone you love or think you will ever again love, you have to take action *before* you take action. By that I mean fucking around marginalizes your value as a person. The other party's behavior has no bearing on that. If you steal you're a thief, if you kill you're a murderer, and if you cheat you're some cheating asshole. This isn't about revenge or your intention to break things off; this is about your person-ness. The only method of dissolving a marriage that requires dishonesty, subterfuge and an airtight alibi is murder. All the other methods can be executed morally. Before we dig into the ways to navigate our once-successful relationship through this, the winter of our discontent, let's take a moment to address the dissolution of a hopeless one. Here's how to end a long-term relationship and maintain your integrity in two simple steps:

1. **Encourage Going to Therapy.** Even if you are 110% sure that it's over, making the overture to see a therapist is the wise move. The potential results of the suggestion can vary widely. For instance, you might be flatly refused! The dialogue might run like this:

    HUSBAND

    Honey? I think we both know how stressful our relationship has been for a while and I feel like we should try to do something to fix it before it's too late. My insurance covers a few couple's therapy sessions, so maybe we could make an appointment?

    WIFE

    What? Are you fucking serious? What the fuck are you even talking about? Where did you learn that shit? You sound like a fucking greeting card! Is it that fucking MIDMEN book I bought you? Is that asshole putting words in your mouth? He was supposed to straighten your fucked-up middle-aged ass out, not tell you how to leave me! Fuck him and fuck you; I'm leaving you first, asshole!

That would certainly put a quick end to things! However, if she takes you up on it, you can move to step two.

2. **Go To Therapy.** Go directly to therapy, do not pass Go, do not keep $200. Even if you believe the dissolution of your marriage is a foregone conclusion, the dissolution of your integrity must not be. Our primary function here is to rid ourselves of the obstacles in our lives that are preventing us from unearthing and indulging in the things that matter to us. Feelings of guilt about how you adjusted your life in what I'll call a *non-wifely* way will create a roadblock between you and your ability to satisfy yourself individually (you just did a masturbation joke in your head, didn't you? What are you, 12?). Integrity in virtually every aspect of your life is huge. If you're the father of kids of any age their impression of the conclusion of your marriage to their mother is going to matter. If they feel that you didn't treat her well, those feelings won't disappear any time soon. This will be the case even if she's horrible to them but especially if she's not. By going to therapy you all but assure that you will be participating in a clean break-up. The easiest way to come out of a traumatic family event like divorce looking like the good guy is to be the good guy.

A byproduct of therapy might also be reconciliation. You may not believe that can happen, maybe you don't even *want* that to happen, but it could happen. You got with this person in the first place for a reason. Unless you or she has changed fundamentally, you may well be the same people you were back then. If a therapist allows you to rediscover each other, then, well, there you are. George Orwell said, "To see what is in front of one's nose needs a constant struggle." Of course he also said, "Not to expose your true feelings to an adult seems to be instinctive from the age of seven or eight onwards," so apparently he's not too confident about your chances in therapy!

If you're married and plan to stay that way, the relationship you have with your significant other lies at the very core of your ability to successfully weather your midlife transition. Dads, of course your kids are your moon and your sky, but the relationship is difficult in some ways, yes? Well, working on that little trapeze act without the net of a trusted partner/wife to catch you makes it considerably harder. Your marriage is probably the single best resource you have to get through this shit and you may well be fucking it up instead of optimizing it. See, this is why you can't have nice things.

Sometimes, of course, you've been just a perfect little angel sent straight from heaven and your mate is being uncool for reasons you can't possibly understand. This requires even more presence of mind and self-control. Don't say what you're thinking about her behavior... at least not in front of young children. Take a moment and consider what's happening then, try just to listen. And not just to the words. You've been together forever; haven't you been watching? What she's saying might have very little to do with what's bothering her. You really don't know shit. So, if she is looking at the couch and bitching about how you left the throw pillows in a pile on the floor, she may really be bothered by her hair feeling like it's drying out as she ages. Anything can mean anything. Writers call it subtext... and so do I. This is the underlying meaning behind actions and statements, etc. The problem is that writers use subtext with an intention. So they know they are using, say, a character mourning the loss of a pet to illustrate that character mourning their own loss of innocence in a larger sense. But in the real world things aren't as nicely crafted. So when your wife gets upset over the way you left the couch pillows, it might be a cry for you to live your life in a more orderly fashion, maybe clean up your garbage dump of a desk, which would be the easy subtext leap, or she might just be taking a hormonal speed bump too fast.

For the MIDMAN, being unable to ascertain the true reason for our wives' behavior (and I think we can agree it's not always *not* our fault) is a serious liability. You can't respond to your wife's couch pillow complaints with, "I'll clean up my desk, I promise," because that's confusing even if it's right. So, we have to get ahead of the game; why is she freaking out about something as marginal as messy couch cushions? It may not have anything to do with you at all. Unfortunately, even if you caringly ask, "What's *really* wrong, honey?" she may not be able to answer. It may be chemical or it may be something so dark, dangerous and heinous that she can't mention it lest she be burned as a witch. So we are placed in a situation where we have to just accept that it's *something* and offer up some attention or consideration in any way we can muster and hope our actions mollify her.

The man who can properly control the wife radius rules the world. As I write this paragraph I am exercising superior wife radius control, literally by the book, given that this is the book. Let me start by saying that notwithstanding a couple of songs so stupid they're genuinely funny, I fucking hate disco music. I don't mean the current version of dance music (though I am capable of producing plenty of hate for that, too), I mean old school, 70s disco. K.C. and the Sunshine Band, for instance. I like most music, rock, pop, swing, klezmer, bebop, whatever, but I fucking hate disco. My wife, however, has wistful roller disco memories for this unspeakable dreck. (I would like to respectfully add at this juncture that I bear no direct animus toward the fine people who plied their trade as musicians polluting the airwaves with this vapor trail of audio poison. You are probably great people and I would party with you. I'd even endure your music to do it. One more thing; down and dirty funk is totally cool.)

As I write, my wife is in the other room spotting. Her mood over the last day or so clearly indicated that a friend of hers would be a-comin' round the mountain when it came. She wasn't being some kind of empusa (if you don't know this word look it up, you'll end up using it yourself as soon as you get an opportunity), she just had that edge. So being an enlightened MIDMAN I left her quietly playing *Words with Friends* in the living room and stepped into my office to give her space. But wait, there's more. I popped over to iTunes and picked out a 70s dance station and cranked it. Fucking disco my friends. K.C. and the Sunshine Band were actually on when I wrote about my disco feelings moments ago. Loud. In my face, which is flanked by my ears. Fuck. Contrary to Mr. Sunshine's assertion, that is NOT the way I like it. If Michael Jackson is the King of Pop, then K.C. is the King of *Stop*! But no Valium, cocktail or herbal remedy would have elevated her mood like a visit from the undead roller boogie spirits.

The lesson we can take away from this sensitive act is one of perspective and balance. Disco sucks, but having a tense wife sucks way more. As I sit here, my wife is quietly scrapbooking on her computer at the desk beside me. Every now and then, when she looks up to cheerfully greet another "song," I know that I have acted wisely. It's 9:24pm and, notwithstanding a nagging desire to take an ice pick to my own eardrums, I have set this evening on a proper trajectory. Okay, the Bee Gees just came on. Fuck this; no more Mr. Nice Guy, we're switching to reggae.

Think ahead, look around. Never assume the obvious to be the truth. Look for the subtext or at least try to counter whatever the cause of your mate's tension might be. You can do this. You just need to get down and boogie, oogie, oogie?

Then there's sexy time. As long as the plumbing works, it's all about dropping a crazy nut. Humans as a species are considered naturally monogamous and naturally promiscuous, depending on who you ask. However, everyone understands that the vast majority of the people they want to fuck don't want to fuck them back, well, everyone but elected members of Congress and professional rappers. The rest of us manage to behave ourselves and have the good taste to wince with self-disapproval when we cross the line with an unwelcome suggestive remark or lingering stare. However, sometimes someone will enter our radius who will actually condescend to fuck us! How we respond to that opportunity is a crucial test of our radius control.

As I mentioned, integrity is one of the key elements of radius control and therefore success. Lying is kryptonite to integrity; it weakens it and makes it speak in halted monosyllables, "Can't-love-self. Must-punish-self. Choices-for-self-must-be-bad." You can pursue the ill-advised fuckage of anyone you'd like but if you're making them fuck a liar, you will make yourself pay. Affairs are the result of complementary circumstances; you're open to having an affair and one becomes available. You may consider an affair because your marriage sucks. If it does, it stands to reason that one or both of you doesn't want to fuck the other one. Then that goes on for a while and, well, a man has needs. You can squeeze one off to relieve blue balls, but blue *ego* balls are another thing. You want to get all manly on something. So you catch the eye of some winsome young thing waiting next to you for her take-out lunch order. The fact that she didn't just turn away from you like you were some kind of wretched, raw fish-chomping Gollum instantly fades your blue ego balls from indigo to robin's egg. That she would actually speak to you gets your X chromosome rubbing together with your Y chromosome like they're dry sticks trying to start a fire. Then maybe lightning strikes or God takes a nap or the entire universe thinks it saw something *over that way* but you actually get this winsome, take-out lunch-eating unfortunate in the sack. What do you get? The *Supernut*™

Fucking somebody else is more than just a nut, it's a Supernut. It's more powerful than a locomotive and often faster than a speeding bullet. It's the stroking of both your ego and your peenie at the same time. (Yes, "peenie." In this example you have a little dick.) But IT IS JUST A NUT! A nut is a nut is a nut. The feeling dwells in our memory no longer than the surfer's memory of catching a wave, or winning a free Jamba Juice on a radio call-in contest or being run over by a powerful locomotive, which is a very short memory indeed. Nothing in your life is worth a simple nut. Nothing. If you're already divorced or just single and have a shot at the boss's hot wife? Don't take it. You'll come out of it without a girlfriend 75% of the time and without a job 100% of the time. You can apply that theory to anything you might jeopardize because you had to go and do that disgusting thing.

Having an affair rates 100% on the *John Edwards How Far up your Ass is Your Head?* scale. There are a lot of things you could say or do while interacting with someone who is not your official someone, but once any part of you slides into any part of them the game changes. Your life is irreversibly affected. All I'm saying is, there are a lot of reasons why someone might be willing to step out as we slog through our middle years, and one of them might legitimately be that you are in the wrong relationship. You have to cop to that and deal with it. There is no time when substantial, important lies are acceptable (you'll notice that I specifically omitted harmless little lies like, "Steve, I loved the book!" from the equation). Compromising *your* integrity in any way diminishes *you*. Fuck everyone else. So no matter what situation you're in, your legitimacy must be defended. Ergo, you have to explore the ending of a relationship legitimately. Let me put it this way; if you're an airline pilot and you're going to crash for whatever reason, you don't just say, "Fuck it, we're going down," and smoke 'em if you got 'em. You try whatever maneuvers or measures you can so you'll be absolutely sure that there's nothing you could have done to prevent it. You can refer to my therapy rule, above. This rule still counts if you are entirely not in love with your spouse and/or believe you are legitimately in love with someone else.

According to the National Center for Family & Marriage Research, even though the overall divorce rate in the U.S. has been dropping since 1991, divorces among Baby Boomers have literally doubled. According to the U.S. Census Bureau, 17.5% of couples over 50 are separated or divorced. That's almost 1 out of 6. In 50-70% of those divorces, infidelity is given as the reason. And if you think it's just us MID*MEN* doing all that stepping out, think again; by all reports the once wide gap between male and female incidents of infidelity is narrowing sharply.

That Chris Rock quote, "*Men* are only as faithful as their options," is a much scarier concept when it's directed toward women! Getting women in bed can be tricky, but getting us all up in there is as easy as getting a bird to shit on your car; all you have to do is wash it. If most women were only as faithful as their options they would live out their lives endlessly rotating through the 64 Kama Sutra sex acts with a million happy strangers.

Sure, we all *want* to do mindless, guiltless, physical fucknastics with pretty much every attractive woman (or dude for my gay brothas) we see in person, in print or on screen. But that doesn't mean we are powerless over our junk. If we're dying to get some strange and our marriage is fine, we have a whole different problem. Truth be told, human beings like some variety in our pants. The mystery of someone new, the thrill of the chase, and the cowardly avoidance of follow-up phone calls; these are all catnip for the sexually active boomer.

The horrifyingly ironic "good" news is that MIDMEN have a diminishing libido. This means our need for sex is still existent and prominent, but the cause may be transitioning. When you were a boy, you were exercising a primitive urge to plant your seed. You were an innocent witness to your own place in evolution. Your reptilian brain was mindlessly driving ever forward; an ignorant general unknowingly sending millions of sperm on a suicide mission in hopes that one brave little hero might breach the enemy line. But now that you're older, the impetus for sex has changed. You are no longer mindlessly driven to reproduce. You want sex for other reasons. Number one is, not surprisingly, because sex is a cool thing to have.

Now let's explore the female side of the libido equation. A woman beyond her prime childbearing years has had her genetic desire to reproduce replaced by other desires, like the desire to be desired, for instance. She's more comfortable with her sexuality, more at ease with her wondrous secret pleasure places. She's gotten past the sexual repression society has conditioned into her and can enunciate, at least to herself, what it is that would satisfy her. In other words; she's horny. It's one of nature's most mischievous little tricks; male sexual desire decreases while female desire increases. Mother Nature has done some great work on mountains and immune systems and stuff, but when it comes to human sexual relationships she can be kind of twat.

Here's how the whole thing goes down for women on a chemical level:

- Around 40ish the lady-folk begin a phase called perimenopause, which you read about earlier with regard to my wife, or as she will be known when she reads this book, my ex-wife.
- Perimenopause is caused by a woman's estrogen level decreasing.
- Estrogen decrease also creates a decrease in binding proteins.
- Women also produce testosterone and the binding proteins prevent free-floating testosterone in the woman's system from binding with cells, but without them the testosterone can "stick" to cells and that causes a reaction.
- The woman, now with the free-floating testosterone doing its thing, suddenly wants to have a lot of sex, just like you would if you still had a lot of testosterone.

There are other theories about why MIDWOMEN get hornier, such as the widely held but fully disproven theory that as compensation for fewer viable eggs, more frequent attempts at fertilization are needed, but no matter what the reason, they do. I'll get deeper into your sex drive in THE BODY, so for now we'll just concentrate on how you can interface successfully with hers. Let's start with one of my annoying little quizzes so that you can assess just how much or little you know about your mate's sexuality. As usual, answer the questions honestly and destroy all evidence.

This quiz is easier than the others, if you consider confronting your almost criminal ignorance of your partner's needs and thoughts "easy." Simply read the statements below and circle the number in front of the ones for which you believe you know the correct answer:

1. My wife likes to watch porn.
2. My wife fantasizes about others while we have sex.
3. My wife enjoys performing oral sex.
4. My wife enjoys having me perform oral sex.
5. My wife does not orgasm.
6. My wife would like to try something "kinky" (i.e., the fuzzy handcuffs or a little spanking or putting objects in your ass that will make great stories for ER staffers).
7. My wife finds other women sexually attractive.
8. My wife masturbates.
9. My wife masturbates your wife. (Sorry, I drifted.)
10. My wife would like more sex with me.
11. My wife has had partners besides me before marriage.
12. My wife has had partners besides me since marriage.

If you're involved in a relationship with great communication, then you probably know the answers to all of these questions. However, unless you and your wife have literally discussed every item on this questionnaire, you're likely guessing or making assumptions about the answers to at least a few of these. I will say this; I actually know the answer to all of these questions as they pertain to my wife and it really helps. If you don't think you know the answers to all of these, you may want to get more curious because you might be missing out on some kooky shit!

Here is what the experts tell us your wife is into:

1. My wife likes to watch porn.

    The prestigious American journal *Fertility and Sterility* published a study by Stanford University School of Medicine, in California, which proved that women like porn as much as men. The 20 women in the study were linked to devices to monitor heart rate, breathing changes and blood flow to their genitals. The women were fully aroused in an average of two minutes. Did they take into consideration that the women might just be turned on by being hooked up to devices?
2. My wife fantasizes about others while we have sex (assuming you're having sex with a wife).

    Seriously? Have you checked yourself out lately? Your hand fantasizes about someone else when you masturbate. Yes she does and if it's around 2015 it's probably George Clooney.
3. My wife enjoys performing oral sex.

    Yes, but not on you. Ever wonder why the gardener stopped charging you? A US-based National Opinion Research Center poll of 3,500 apparent liars found that only 17% of women actually enjoyed or were enthusiastic about performing fellatio. But women still perform it more often than they receive oral sex. Raise a glass to the ladies.
4. My wife enjoys having me perform oral sex.

    That same study found that only 34% of men and 29% of women found cunnilingus "very appealing." With all due respect to the National Opinion Research Center, I think you've been sold a bill of goods on this one. I am given to the belief that if people end up in a sexual situation they will willingly stick each other into one another's mouth. So, assume your wife is in the 29%.

5. My wife does not orgasm.

   She does with me! (high five) Planned Parenthood (as published in *Women's Day Magazine*) reports that 30% of women have trouble achieving an orgasm. I can't speak for the accuracy of this statistic, but I can say that orgasms matter and if your wife isn't having them and you don't know it, there is a serious communication problem in your relationship. The ability to bring your wife to orgasm might be the most helpful arrow you have in your quiver (yes, in this example you have a metaphorical arrow to compensate for your "peenie" from the previous example) to make your house a home. Remember this; during orgasm is the only time she can't hate you even if she wants to. She's not even thinking about you. *#GeorgeClooney*

6. My wife wants to try something kinky.

   I did some Google searching and found some survey results on WebMD, which they lifted from *Woman's Day*. The results are decisive: your lady is a stone cold freak. Here are some of their findings:

   - Touch themselves while you watch – 80% yes.
   - Bondage – 66% cuffs, 74% spanked, 63% hair pulling (but take your time. You can't just slap the cuffs on her then start hitting her and pulling her hair. That's not a sex session, that's an arrest.).
   - She wants to use sex toys – see cuffs above and add some.
   - Public sex – Yes (though she may just be trying to get herself arrested. See Bondage above).

7. My wife finds other women attractive.

   Having another woman join you scored 25% (couldn't access data on another guy, but the forums reflect some serious enthusiasm).

8. My wife masturbates.

   Yes. *Fifty Shades of Grey* has sold more than 70 million copies worldwide, and it wasn't for the artistry of the prose, youknowhatImsayin?

9. My wife masturbates your wife

   25% chance my friend...

10. My wife would like more sex with me.

    Studies suggest that more than 60% of wives want as much if not more sex than their man.

11. My wife has had partners besides me before marriage.

    In 2011 it was reported that a women's median number of sex partners is four. The median number of partners for men was 7. Of course if men *reported* a median number of 7, the actual number is 4.

12. My wife has had partners besides me since marriage.

    Twenty-nine percent of MIDMEN and 16% of their MIDWIVES admitted to cheating. Gen X is about the same for women, with men coming in about 9% lower.

Knowing more about your wife or partner sexually is of the utmost importance if you'd like the relationship to continue, or maybe even flourish. But women are mysterious and men can be incurious. Being present mentally is pretty much the most viable way to collect the information you need to successfully participate in your primary relationship. For instance, my wife uses Laura Mercier foundation make-up. She also likes Manhattans more than Rob Roys, loves octopus almost any way you prepare it, and would be very happy if she never had to watch another magician (which is sad since I have a disproportionate number of close friends who are excellent magicians). My knowing these things is a clear indication that I was paying attention to her and not just trying to reverse engineer the conversation after she says, "Are you paying attention to me?" Conversely, not knowing things about her that matter indicates to her that you're really not into her. If you know that A-Rod was suspended for using Biogenesis but you didn't know your wife climaxes clitorally, she has every right to be pissed.

You don't have to sit down with a survey questionnaire to learn about your wife, though that could be fun:

You (dropping into a chair across from hers)

Okay, I'm going to ask you a couple of questions. One, do you have any special interests?

Her (pausing the TV)

What?

You (calm)

I thought it would be good if I knew some details about what's important to you. Do you have any special interests?

Her

Oh, come on. It's that fucking MIDMEN book again, right?

You

It doesn't matter why I'm asking, it's just important that—

Her

Listen ass-wad, I'm about done with you and your little book, okay? If you gave a flaming shit about me I wouldn't

> have to answer some fucking vapid pre-fab questions; you would already know the answers. You want to know my special interest? I'm interested in you getting the fuck out of my face. . . NOW!

So, don't start getting all inquisitive, just start paying attention.

Chapter 5

THE KIDS

"Everybody knows how to raise children, except the people who have them."

P. J. O'Rourke

I'm not going to lie to you; I don't have kids. And you're not going to lie to me; you're a little jealous. Virtually all of my friends have kids so I have a fair understanding of the different ways kids can be accepted, endured, adored, nurtured, etc. by their parents but I totally lack the genetic connection one naturally has with their progeny. That said, having things running smoothly with your kids could be a determining factor in your ability to suss out what matters to you and then infuse your life with it. You require a clear mind to pursue your muse, especially if your muse is a clear mind (am I right yogis?). Your relationship with your kids is a big deal in the clearheaded-ness biz. So please accept the next few pages of pretty commonly understood childrearing techniques as my way of addressing a very important topic for MIDMEN without my having any actual expertise on the subject or desire to do in-depth research (i.e. reproduce). If there's something in here you didn't already know, or needed a reminder on, great. If not, I'll try to jack it up with the kind of sparkling wit that has made the book up until now tolerable enough to get you here.

To introduce my little omnibus of childrearing advice (largely pilfered from Web MD to which I am now extending credit), I will use a stupid game.

I have created two columns of entries. The column on the left is a list of problems you may encounter while raising your teenager. The column on the right is a list of solutions. You see where I'm headed; use your handy #2 pencil to connect the problem with the solution. I'm concentrating on problems with teens for two reasons: first, younger kids don't pose the same level of problem because you may actually still be able to take them in a fair fight; and second, if you're a MIDMAN, then either your kids are teens or your younger kids are probably from your second marriage so we'll assume you already know what you're doing. As always, the page will self-destruct five seconds after you have put your pencil down. Begin.

	PROBLEM		SOLUTION
1.	Your teen seems to hate you	A.	Be understanding; listen.
2.	Kid is addicted to computer/phone/ tablet/game	B.	Really not much you can do. Seek professional help.
3.	Kid is staying out too late	C.	Stay calm and weather the storm.
4.	Hanging out with kids you don't like	D.	Make sure your rules are in line with other parents' and then enforce them.
5.	Drama Queen (largely for daughters, but...)	E.	Put some limitations in place, then enforce them.

Are your answers locked in? Okay. Let's see how you did.

Since the solutions column delivers all the specificity of the Magic 8-Ball answers, you might have found this test more challenging than you expected. But there are actually some subtle differences. Don't bother scoring yourself here, though if you got them all wrong you may want to fake your own death and change your identity so the kids can find more suitable stewardship.

Here are the correct answers: 1 = C, 2 = E, 3 = D, 4 = B, 5 = A

Now let's take the problems and solutions and look at them individually.

1. **Your teen seems to hate you/Stay calm and weather the storm.**

   Actually, there are a couple of schools of thought on why pretty much all teenage kids rebel against their parents to varying degrees. The one I like is the one that makes the friction seems less personal. It's based on a London study that found a possible link to a temporary form of autism in teenagers. Basically, the study, conducted by Professor David Skuse of University College (or was it *College University*?) suggests that teens' pissy behavior is the result of an autistic disability. Since the body is in a period of expedited growth during puberty, the brain is also undergoing drastic change. The prof called it a "rewiring." Their ability to comprehend the needs of those around them through traditional communication like facial expressions seems to all but disappear. He believes this is a result of the brain reorganizing itself toward adulthood.

If you accept that there's a chemical change taking place, then you can maintain a livable détente without harboring resentment. Think about it like this: if someone walks up to you, sticks their finger down their throat and projectile vomits on you, that is totally not cool and you are well within your rights to dislike that person. Actually, I think the "Stand Your Ground" law lists that as a shootable offense. But if someone you're talking to suddenly turns sheet white and Old Faithfuls an overenthusiastic visit to a taco bar onto your face, you're not going to be happy about it, but you can't really fault the ailing party. You might wish they had better reflexes or aim, but, c'mon, they're sick. If you can view your teen as chemically fucked up instead of just fucked up, it will help.

2. **Kid is addicted to electronics/Put some limitations in place, then enforce them.**

Based on the stories (read: complaints) I hear from my MIDMEN friends who are fathers, pretty much all of whom have teens or tweens, their kids have disappeared into the "down and in" world of their Smartphones and never so much as poke their heads into the "up and out" world of the actual world world. Being forced to cohabitate with the tops of their progeny's heads because they are bowing to the Smartphone gods infuriates these dads. Even though these guys are legitimately pissed, they can't really do much about it because they seem to harbor some belief that their kids have an "opinion" and require "respect." Of course they do to an extent, but this isn't about that; it's about calming your mind and making the world a better place for you – radius control stuff. So how do you deal with it? Well, with-it parents who are in the know (are *groovy*! When did 1972 break out?) are making good use of their kids' technology addictions by selectively limiting it and granting it for discipline.

Here's how it works. Pretend that the kid is into smoking crack instead of addicted to computers. Now put yourself in the role of your kid's crack dealer (in this example your name is Santiago Mateo Jimenéz aka "El Mofeta Jimenéz" and you suck your gold eye tooth absently when you're thinking). Since they crave the rock and you have the rock, you can get them to do anything. So, if they do well, they get some pipe; they do bad, they go cold sweats for a while. After a few applications of the rules, you've got the kid turned out. In essence, *you* are the kid's Smartphone pimp! You probably bought them the phone, pay the bills for the data plan and the electricity that powers it. That means you can literally shut off any aspect of service, from the cell service to the electricity to the kid's room, or flat-out cancel the service or implement the indelicate if highly efficient "sledge hammer technique," which is what El Mofeta would do.

3. Kid is staying out too late/Be like other parents.

Here's one of those areas where real life parenting experience is mandatory and I am lacking it. My old friend, veteran comic Nick Carmen Cosentino, had an illuminating Facebook posting. He wrote something that by his own admission only an actual parent might understand. He said that when his grown kid is going away for any extended period, a parent could find "…at least momentary relief for your aching heart, if you go into their closet and smell their clothes." There is no way to put together this chapter without acknowledging that bond between parent and child. Speaking to this aspect of parenting from the perspective of the childless (as far as I know, wink, wink) is a dispassionate exercise.

Anxiety caused by a kid staying out too late is a singular problem because it is so perfectly born of love for the kid. They're out late and you worry. You worry because you love them and you can't bear the thought of something happening to them. Assuming you deal with "Hanging Out with Kids You Don't Like" as outlined below, the experts kind of want you to suck this one up a little bit, or at least punt. Basically they want you to follow the parent pack and try and put your curfew rules in line with theirs. If you aren't already in touch with your kids' friends' parents, this is a nice reason to break the ice. Get phone numbers and form some kind of "I don't want to actually be your friend, I just want to be able to track down my kid when I need to" friendship. However, if rules are established and the kid breaks them, go for the Smartphone or whatever your kid's metaphorical crack happens to be.

4. **Hanging out with kids you don't like/Seek professional help.**

The general consensus among parenting experts is that your kid doesn't hang out with kids who are too different from them. If you think your kid is hanging out with dirt bags, their parents are thinking the same thing, but in their thoughts your kid is one of the dirt bags. Because of the autism thing or other teen-related behavior disorders discussed above, you are really in a tough spot on this one. If you tell them their friends are dirt bags they will defend them against you. If you tell them that they will end up getting in trouble, they won't believe you. So you need to address this from a very pragmatic position. God help me for disagreeing with some experts on this one, but I have to believe there is something you can do.

Since ongoing discourse with a belligerent teen can be a ferocious radius control buzzkill, I would like to recommend the "fake it 'til you make it" plan. I know I don't have kids, but I was one and a little lowlife at that. The "fake it 'til you make it" plan is essentially the system my mother had me operate under and look how I turned out (*what*?). Assuming you have embraced the computer addict/crack dealer discipline system or some viable manner of authority enforcement like motor vehicle control (are you the insurance policy holder? POWER!), you can lay down the social rule thusly: "You, my little friend, are being parentally supervised. Until you move out, you will be observed. If you fuck up, one of two things will happen. If I catch you, I will punish you in some way and if the law catches you, they will punish you in some way. If you get arrested, I will let the law deal with you. If you get hurt, you will experience pain. So do all the shit I can't stop you from doing, but if you don't hide it really well, you'll pay the price." The very act of maintaining the appearance of a clean nose will go a long way toward your kids actually keeping their noses clean. A weekend in jail facing felony charges can also be pretty persuasive (for the record, my mom did end up hiring me a decent lawyer in time for arraignment).

5. **Drama Queen/Be understanding; listen.**
   This may be frustrating, but there really is nothing you can do. You can't marginalize your kid's feelings even if they make no sense to you. How can you possibly even understand what matters deeply to them? You were a teen more than a quarter of a fucking century ago! Your priorities are things like paying bills and trying to find some kind of productive place of mental and physical satisfaction so you can enjoy what's left of your time on Earth before the inevitable catches up with you and kills you dead; *dead*! Do you think she can relate to those? Of course not. So if you don't happen to have a crush on a boy who doesn't even know you're alive, or a friend who tweeted some awful lie about you, shut up and listen for a while. Then try a hug. *That's* radius control!

If you're estranged from your family, you still have to play by all the same rules. There is no amount of geography that can separate you from your parental obligations. They live in your mind and manifest in the form of guilt, drinking and spoiling those other, newer kids who popped out of your second marriage (which may just have been an attempt to solve your midlife crisis). Knowing that there are people in the world who are hurting as a result of your inability to man up and be dad will fuck with you until the day you die. My father (not his real name) who divorced my mother when I was about 12 does not speak to me. I tried to reconnect but he's a troubled man in many ways and can't muster the courage to reconcile. Truth be told, he didn't even raise me, he just kind of rubbed off on me. In my opinion, and probably in your kid's opinion, if you're on my father's side of this equation you're screwing yourself out of a great friendship. Unless you're a total sociopath you can't just walk away from your fatherly connection to your kids. It exists on a cellular level. So put on your big boy toupee and call or write or something. You will punish yourself in one way or another if you don't. Roy F. Baumeister, whose beefy, 'roid-infused PhD soundly thrashes my skinny little GED, wrote in *Psychology Today* that "...many of these men agonize and suffer over the loss of their family." Agony does not equate with happiness unless you're Frank, the freaky dude in the first *Hellraiser* who smiled and said, "Jesus wept," before being blissfully ripped apart by meat hooks.

The U.S. Census Bureau reports a total of 24 million children in America. One out of three of those kids doesn't have a biological father in their home. The National Fatherhood Initiative published an interesting report about being raised with a father in the home versus not. Though the report doesn't consider that *not* having the father in the home might have its advantages, for instance if the father is an asshole (coughing into hand, "*Mine.*"), it did reveal a trend. I should mention that this particular study involved 134 children of adolescent mothers over the first ten years of life. But what researchers found was that father-child contact indicated "...better socio-emotional and academic functioning." The children who had engaged fathers were better behaved and even had higher reading scores.

Since my father is still alive and has comported himself irresponsibly with regard to his obligation to father, I can speak with some authority. If you had an absentee father for all or much of your life, you understand what they robbed you of. It's not just wishful thinking that leads us to assume they are living miserable lives with their fear, irresponsibility, and self-hatred eating them up from the inside like a cancer. The experts tell us they really are. If you are that guy and you'd like to clear the way to find what really matters in your life and pursue it, I have a great idea: don't be that guy.

Chapter 6

THE FOLKS

"Age is a cruel mistress. So is my Dominatrix, Miss Leah, but age doesn't have a safe word."

Steve Ochs GED

THE FOLKS

MIDMEN born in 1965 will themselves turn 65 in 2030. That same year, their parents should be dancing around the edges of 90. It won't be a particularly pretty dance to watch, but dance they will. Historically, how we have interacted with our parents may have little to do with how we'll be implicated into their lives as they age beyond self -care. The relationship we have with our parents has more than likely been, and always will be, one of the most complicated of our lives. The variations on how each individual relates or interacts with his or her parents are so infinite that any attempt by a book to try and offer generalized advice is no more than a fool's errand. So let's dig in.

I have a composite friend I'll call Cyril. Cyril is a creative type. For his whole life, which is roughly how long I knew him, he dedicated himself to artistic pursuits. From theater to music to art, Cyril couldn't help but create. He actually earned a living with various manifestations of his aesthetically eager mind. School wasn't his thing but he went. He even logged some college time, albeit begrudgingly.

Relationships were a challenge for him. Not just friendly relationships, though I'll never forget the time he and a friend mugged me at gun point, finally giving themselves away by laughing raucously behind their masks. Science note: while laughter is contagious, two big fucking guns in your face have been proven an effective immunization. It's the only case of an infectious condition that can be cured if the subject so much as *thinks* he's going to get a shot for it. Cyril had trouble relating to other people. He was a loner, a drug enthusiast, a brawler, and an amateur drinker, even though his experience should have made him a pro. As a friend he always had your back but ultimately rejected your heart. There was something wrong deep down inside Cyril. This became more evident the longer I knew him and, having known him as a teen, I had some clues as to what that might have been. I don't have pictures, but I believe he suffered some form of physical abuse when we were kids. I also believe, and again, I have no solid evidence to prove it, his father was implicated, most likely as an accessory after the fact. The most damning evidence of this abuse was that he did what so many abuse victims eventually do; he took his own life.

This is where things get complicated enough to be in a book. His father had died slowly of a terminal illness. Cyril was called upon to provide him with care, which included literally carrying his wasted body into treatment rooms (this book just gets funnier and funnier, doesn't it?). Meanwhile, his mother, who turned a blind eye to any untoward goings on in the house for Cyril's entire life, was herself going dotty. So Cyril, with a vast history of trauma at the hands of these people, was now their primary caretaker. The most shocking aspect of his call to duty was his answering it!

Cyril's father eventually died. Then, a few years later, his mother did the same. Cyril, who had married a wonderful woman and attentively raised three exceptional kids, could have lived happily ever after. But he couldn't shake the traumas of his childhood. He had breakdowns and hospital stays and prescriptions for medications and even had a remarkably high IQ with which to work out his mental troubles but nothing worked. You can blindfold your eyes and plug your ears, but there's only one way to shut down your brain completely, and he went for it.

Why? Why would someone, whose life was so despoiled by his parents that he was finally driven to take his own life, dedicate himself to their care? One reason might have been something called "filial responsibility," which is the name for actual laws that demand that offspring care for their *on*spring. According to *The New York Times*, 28 states currently have them. Sixteen of these can come after you for actual money! Eight of them have refusal on the books as a crime and can arrest or imprison you for parental neglect. Four states can do both. That said, almost half of the filially proactive states have never enforced their responsibility laws. And even if they were to try, there are defenses. If you can prove you can't afford it, or as in Cyril's case, it can be proved that the parents abandoned you or had "unclean hands," meaning had done the child some wrong, then the progeny is off the hook.

But that's not why he stepped up. He stepped up for the same reason all of my friends with shitty parents have ultimately stepped up. It's because our relationship with our parents, and by extension our siblings, is rooted far more deeply than our feelings might indicate. We have behavioral habits that are profoundly instilled. Our parents' voices were likely the predominant sound we heard in our formative years. That's hard to shake. When those voices call out for help, we respond. That tends to be the case whether they responded to our calls for help or not. So Cyril, whose cries, silent or otherwise, went unanswered by his parents, still answered theirs. When it comes to radius control, parents have got us by the short hairs.

Whether these reflexive responses are the result of nature or nurture is a tough one, but I believe that even if we disdain our parents outwardly, somewhere in our conditioning or maybe our DNA, there's a connection. I'm experiencing a really good example of that in my own life as I write, but this isn't an autobiography, so butt out.

Assuming your parents are alive, you're likely being saddled with some aspect of their care or soon will be. It doesn't matter if they were a dream or a nightmare. They either have become, or will become, less independent. While I am not currently experiencing the pressures of parental care, I know that it's just around the corner. By "just around the corner" I mean the place where I plan to hide so that I can spring out unexpectedly in front of them and yell, *Boo!* thereby significantly shortening my tenure as caretaker. Many of my friends are already deep in the process of *parenting their parents*. Some of them have parents who need money but are physically okay, some don't need money but have debilitating conditions, some have no physical problems and lots of money but can't remember where they put it.

Dr. Mark Frankel, is the president and CEO of Taking Care Inc., a Canadian organization that helps people like us understand parental care. Most of those who haven't entered the process of parental care yet just figure we'll visit and call exactly as much as our genuine desire or guilt requires until our parents get so old they need to be shipped off to the closest ElderWood Senior Care facility.* He explains that going into long-term care is not an isolated event; it's usually a gradual process with many stops and bumps along the way. It starts with a feeling of disorientation, difficulty remembering what they were talking about or a mysterious ache. (Oh fuck, I just described me!) Then it expands to certifiable chronic health problems or physical challenges. As the situation(s) grow more pronounced, the kids are incrementally engaged. Suddenly a ride to a doctor's appointment followed by a trip to their favorite soup joint becomes researching home care providers followed by complaints that the home care provider we chose for them steals.

So Frankel developed a five-stage framework that outlines what our parents will endure when they get "up there." Not only has his framework made dealing with an aging parent easier for who-knows-how-many people, it's also made writing this chapter easier for me. The framework is his; the titles of the stages and shitty jokes are mine.

Stage 1 – It's All Good

If you're at the beginning or even a little ways into your MIDMEN period, your folks are probably in stage 1. They're still driving, they're feeding themselves just fine and bickering like there's no tomorrow. They probably don't even want your support, unless it's to take their side in the bickering:

* ElderWood is the actual name of a chain of senior care facilities, which one must assume was ironically chosen given the rarity of its occurrence.

DAD

I had to (undecipherable word that sounds like "poach,") the damn car!

MOTHER

What are you talking about "poach the car?" What does that mean?

DAD

I didn't say, "Poach the car." Who poaches a car?!

MOTHER

You did so say poach the car! Scotty, did your father just say, "Poach the car?"

SCOTT

I don't want to get in the middle—

MOTHER

It's a simple question, did he or did he not say, "Poach the car?"

SCOTT

I'm sorry dad, but, um, you kind of did.

DAD

PARK!!! Are you people idiots? I said park the god-damn car! What, do you want toast with the car, now!? (Mumbling to self, loudly enough to be heard) Poach the car...

MOTHER

Well, it sounded like poach to us.

During stage 1 the MIDMEN's concentration should be on making himself available and visiting often enough to spare himself from harsh self-scrutiny in the later stages, or what I call investing in radius control futures.

Stage 2 – If You Insist

This is the short, living limbo before the long, dead limbo. The MIDMEN's parents (or MIDLAWS, or both, as the case may be) are still doing pretty well, but should you ask if you can help with something, they'll probably let you. And if you don't ask, they'll manipulate you into asking and when you do, they'll let you. I'm just talking about little shit like some shopping or moving stuff around their house. Since the aging process is unlikely to reverse, take this as a shot across the bow. Things are going to get harder for them before they get easier, and the progress of the slow down could accelerate rapidly without notice.

This would be a good time to start planning for the next three stages. For instance, even though the folks are getting around okay, you may want to start looking for someplace more accommodating for them to live. Earlier in the book you read about Del Webb's "active adult" communities. Those aren't what they'll need. Del Webb is intended for active adults over 55. (Oh, fuck; that's me again!)

The type of place you'll need to start familiarizing yourself with is also NOT assisted living. Okay, it is… but not really. The kind of facilities that should be investigated are known as *senior residences designed for independent living.* These are places where people get their own actual apartment but also feature security, food, cleaning and laundry. Basically, it's an all-inclusive resort where your folks can spend one last long, glorious vacation. Again, stage 2 is not the time to move them yet, just time for you to learn what's out there.

Stage 3 – I've Fallen and I Can't Get Up!

Okay, NOW it's time to move them… or hire some help to visit the house… or create a regular schedule for yourself so you can help out. My mom is a spry and self-sufficient 80, and my stepdad, just a few years behind her, still skips down the street when provoked. However, I can recall my grandmother at their age leaving a jar of applesauce in the fridge for so long that when I opened it the fungus said, "Hi Steve."

Stage 3 can usually be addressed with a couple of simple moves. Getting them a Life Alert, the brand advertised by the slogan in the subsection title, is a nice way of attaining peace of mind. If they've worked out the mobile phone thing, great, but you may want to put your hands on it and make sure that things like 911 and your sibling's phone number(s) are on speed dial.

If you're an only child, you're already volunteered for all duties. But if your parents have more than one child, it could be a blessing or a curse. Sometimes everyone falls into line, optimizing his or her respective skills sets. One sibling might have the time and geographical proximity to offer boots on the ground for onsite assistance and the other can provide financial or logistical support. I'll use myself as an example, but I'll call myself Neville to protect my family's privacy.

Neville is very close emotionally to his mother Esther and stepdad, Lloyd, who he will call Agnes and Bucky. His sister Lori, who Neville will call Tess, is also emotionally close, but much closer geographically. Neville and his wife, Julie, who he will from here on out refer to as Judy, run a small business about thirty-five miles away and would require about an hour to get to Agnes and Bucky's (due to the 405 nightmare through the Sepulveda Pass, for my LA, CA peeps), while Tess is only blocks away and, if she's not at work, could be there in five minutes. So, it would stand to reason that she would answer a "boots on the ground" call. Meanwhile, Neville and Judy can be relied upon to, um, you know, um… okay, bad example.

Anyway, there is no reason to wait until the shit hits the fan for siblings to work out who is going to be doing what. If one of you has domestic skills and the other has investigative skills (for things like exploring which facility would be best for stage 4 and 5) then your duties are easily sorted. If not, then you're in for the kind of petty squabbling you probably haven't engaged in since you were teens. It's a tough conversation to begin with. As we discussed back in THE REASON, we confirm our own mortality through the mortality of our parents. By extension, this means we also view Simple Truth 2, *It's ultimately going to suck*, through the same lens. Our parents don't want to get old and less capable, but their time has come and that's that. We don't want to experience the downside of aging, but we're attempting to accept it, or at least not let it interfere with our Simple Truth 3: *Tough shit. I will still need to live life to the fullest until I can't anymore*. But who the hell knows how our siblings are going to react? If we're lucky we have one who's a control freak and all we'll have to do is make visits or scrape together a little cash now and then (are you reading this, Tess?). Okay, I just read that back and it seems like I'm suggesting that MIDMEN want to do as little as possible for their aging parents or are estranged or aloof or are just dicks. But of course that's ridiculous. It is, right?

Having had no previous experience in elder care, MIDMEN are probably ill prepared for handling the rigors of parenting our parents, so here's a laundry list of some of the more common shit you may need to deal with:

-**Getting around**. This is one of the first areas where our parents are likely to need an assist in stage 3. The AAA says that people tend to outlive their ability to drive safely by 7-10 years. What the AAA doesn't mention is that they'll be spending those 7-10 years in front of me in an intersection waiting for a written invitation to make a left. The diminished driving skills aren't necessarily because their judgment or reflexes are failing. It could be arthritis, medications of the "do not operate machinery" variety, limited flexibility, etc. At a certain point, they're wise not to gamble on driving because they've grown more frail, and an accident that would just bruise a younger person could really fuck them up good. If you or a family member can't get them around when they need gettin' and cabs are too expensive or complicated, there are services like Uber or Lyft, which keep a credit card on file so no cash ever changes hands. This could be your credit card so you can pump money into the situation and absolve yourself of some deeply rooted guilt. But if you go that way, the folks (or *folk* as the case may be) will need to have a Smartphone and enough tech smarts to use an app.

Another thing to look into is Dial-A-Ride Paratransit services (ADA/DAR). The program is part of the Americans with Disabilities Act and most cities seem to have one. I spent about five minutes searching the net and found three different ways I could get around my city if I were a senior, one of which was a free door-to-door service. The regular buses were just $1.50.

Two final comments: hitchhiking is never acceptable and *wandering off* is not a form of transportation.

-Medical Advocacy. Your mommy and/or daddy (yes, in this example you're suffering from arrested development) are likely seeing some doctors about this or that. Having someone there to look out for their best interests is, you know, in their best interest. Even if it's just for show, having a concerned party on hand can remind health professionals to bring their A game. You may also find that your involvement has to go deeper than a symbolic presence. A little homework may be required for you to make sure your parent(s) are getting the correct care. My wife had an extremely rare syndrome caused by the severing of a parasympathetic nerve. The doctors were pretty much useless, but I was able to find the only other case out there and the treatment used by the only doctor to develop a treatment to treat it, and a local doctor treated her with the treatment and the treatment proved successful!*

* Treatment.

Then there is the issue of coverage. Insurance companies are not famous for reminding doctors to bill them, so determining what coverage covers what and what benefits your folks are entitled to falls to the primary guardian. Having more than one form of coverage can sometimes be more confusing than having just one, so sorting this stuff out is a nightmare the kids have to face. The "good" news is that your folks may already be covered by Medicare. If they're not eligible, then look into Obamacare (the Affordable Health Care Act). This may be a preferable choice as many government programs will require your parents be completely "spent down" to receive benefits… and I believe that's your legacy they'd be spending. Finally, some real incentive to act!

-Medication dispensation. Who could forget that classic Schoolhouse Rock ditty? This may not be scientifically proven, but it would seem that people add one pill, four times a day, for every decade they live. This means that by the time they're, say, seventy, they're taking seven pills four times a day. Okay, that's a generalization and an exaggeration (another line from the Schoolhouse Rock ditty), but people do tend to have several prescriptions they need to take on a precise schedule. But what are the odds that the country that developed a pill for everything didn't invent a way to get them into the patient on time?

There are a whole bunch of models of something called an Automatic Pill Dispenser. Ticking away like the *60 Minutes* TV show bumpers or the kitchen timer that counts down your next experiment in the ancient art of arterial cloggery, pill dispensers now have timers. There are countless varieties of these things on the market, but essentially they all do the same thing: give a pill taker the pills they need to take and let them know when it's time to take them.

The variations on the pill timer theme are just as robust: mobile phone apps, key chains, vibrating watches, Internet connected pill bottles and even preternaturally gifted drug mules who can regurgitate a condom containing a correct dose of meds at the precise time they're needed; the list is endless. Your albatross, I'm sorry; your *cherished elder* is likely on one med or another (and another), and not taking them appropriately can cause some serious shit. Because there is sometimes more than one doctor prescribing, things can get confused. There are interactions to look out for and even redundancy since generic drugs have different names from the original on which they're based and each other. Here's an example. The brand name for Clonazepam is Klonopin, but not only is the drug available as a generic; it's a "pam," which are essentially the class including happy pills. They include: Albraolam, Lorazepam, Diazepam, Clozapine, Temazepam, Clorazepate, Clorazepate Diptassim, Clobazam, Oxazepam, Chlordiazepoxide, Chlordiazepoxide Hydrochloride, Midazolam, Triazolam, Flurazepam, Estazolam, Flumazenil, Chlordiazepoxide/Clidnium bromide, Chlordiazepoxide/Amitrtyline and, of course, Flurizide Hydrochloride, "the cute one." Do you think your folks would be able to determine the difference and/or similarity between these things? I can, but only because I attend tastings. So, someone taking any of these drugs is double dosing if they take it with any of the others. Messing up with meds can turn a normal situation into a hospital stay and a subsequent rehab. Think having a parent involved in that would make your radius any more controllable? Can you say, "Fuck no?"

-Home is Where the Heart Medication Is. At a certain point, the visits and advocating won't be enough. Activities that were once referred to as *things* are suddenly categorized as *problems.* It may become necessary for your parents to change their address. This gives flight to two potentially huge issues. First, they may not want to move. Having some information about an attractive potential residence or two is probably smart when broaching the subject.

Second, what are they leaving behind? A rent controlled apartment? A house? Three rooms of furniture? A hoarder's grotto of rat urine-soaked newspaper stacks? Many a family has been torn apart by siblings getting grabby on the folks' stuff. What your folks will need to do if they haven't already is prepare the paperwork that will survive them, such as a revocable trust. For instance, they have to be prepared to name a beneficiary or beneficiaries. Property, including financial assets, that lists a transfer on death beneficiary (TOD), or a pay on death beneficiary (POD), will go directly to the named beneficiary. Motor vehicles have to be listed, savings accounts – in fact all accounts – and of course, real estate. The term Pro-Bait is easily acceptable to MIDMEN when it refers to the shack that sells double crossing fish snacks for anglers, but *probate* is a little more daunting. Basically, probate is our government's method of squeezing the last out of us after we're dead. If your parents, or you for that matter, haven't created a will and/or trust, you *will* be brutally taxed before distribution of assets after death. Ironically, the very government that ransacks those accounts has made a comprehensive guide to stop them from doing so available. Visit http://www.usa.gov/topics/money/personal-finance/trusts.shtml and learn what you need to do to keep your parents stuff in the family and out of the US Treasury.

The great thing about preparing these documents is that is it removes the impetus for rivalry and discourse. For crying out loud, you're a MIDMAN in the process of creating an environment where you can manifest what matters to you. Engaging in some familial squabbling with your blood relations isn't helpful. But even with a trust in place, it may also be unavoidable. The best thing you can do is remain even, calm and--

I'm sorry; I'm getting something in my earpiece. What's that you say? Really, he's in the book right now? Wow, great. Okay, reader, big news. Rudyard Kipling just wandered into the book! Apparently, he wandered out of Gungha Din to get some water, which probably wasn't the smartest move, but he stumbled into my humble little book! Please welcome to the page, Rudyard Kipling! It's great to see you Rudy. Tell me you'll do a little something for us, maybe a poem? Hey, would you do "If" for us? It would fit this part of the book so perfectly. Yes? Wow! Ladies and MIDMEN, please give it up for Rudyard Kipling!

"If you can keep your head when all about you
Are losing theirs and blaming it on you,
If you can trust yourself when all men doubt you,
But make allowance for their doubting too;
If you can wait and not be tired by waiting,
Or being lied about, don't deal in lies,
Or being hated, don't give way to hating,
And yet don't look too good, nor talk too wise:
If you can dream - and not make dreams your master;
If you can think - and not make thoughts your aim;
If you can meet with Triumph and Disaster
And treat those two impostors just the same;
If you can bear to hear the truth you've spoken
Twisted by knaves to make a trap for fools,
Or watch the things you gave your life to broken,
And stoop and build 'em up with wornout tools:
If you can make one heap of all your winnings
And risk it on one turn of pitch-and-toss,
And lose, and start again at your beginnings
And never breathe a word about your loss;
If you can force your heart and nerve and sinew
To serve your turn long after they are gone,
And so hold on when there is nothing in you
Except the Will which says to them: 'Hold on!'
If you can talk with crowds and keep your virtue,
Or walk with kings - nor lose the common touch,
If neither foes nor loving friends can hurt you,

If all men count with you, but none too much;
If you can fill the unforgiving minute
With sixty seconds' worth of distance run -
Yours is the Earth and everything that's in it,
And - which is more - you'll be a MIDMAN my son!"

Wow! Please, let's give it up, *MC Ruddy K in the Bizzy, yo!* And, man did he nail it, or what? Come see us again in the sequel, won't you?

As we enter into circumstances of conflict, especially with those we can't just disregard, we have to keep our emotions on a short leash and our logic on a long one. Even if your siblings can't grasp the concept, this isn't about you; it's about your folks. The first selfless step is more frequent visits, conscious observation of your parents' behaviors and capabilities, patience and the initiation of impossible conversations about things like living wills, trusts and final directives such as an Advance Health Care Directive.

Stage 4 – Hello Muddah, Hello Faddah, Here You Are in Camp Seniorah

Okay; enough is enough. It's time for the folks to eschew the luxuries of 100% independence and the indignities of climbing stairs in favor of a safer, more convenient lifestyle. This means it's time to move them to that senior residence I described above. Bear in mind, this is not a nursing home by any manner of description. This isn't about the meds, the beds or rolling out the deads. In fact, a lot of these places have game rooms, field trips, transportation to local shopping, pools and wild sex orgies. Okay, maybe not orgies but singles can easily find themselves doing some serious flirting and maybe more at these places. Men have a clear advantage in this area. According to an article in the Scientific American, by age 85 there are about six women to every four men. This provides a little good news for MIDMEN; if you follow the health advice coming up in THE BODY, you stand a good chance of finally getting that three-way with two chicks you've always dreamed of. One quick request from everyone who will be younger than you when and if that happens; no pictures, please! However, should you manage to get your deeply grooved groove on, be careful! The Centers for Disease Control, or *CDC*, report that venereal diseases among seniors are skyrocketing. Brace yourself; from 2007 to 2011, Syphilis increased 52% and Chlamydia increased by 31%. (Coughing into my hand, "*Viagra*.")

If we're really lucky our parents or parent already prepared for this eventuality with long term care insurance or other safeguards. If both parents are still with us and with each other, they may be in different stages of their campaign against the armies of minutes that so vastly outnumber them. Or maybe one of your folks has already passed and the other is winding down. Either way, it's time to follow the path that provides the highest quality of life for all involved: your parents, your siblings and you. And, hey, think about this you selfish bastard; the three simple truths may be geared toward those of us still in the full flower of health and productivity, but it doesn't mean your parents shouldn't be entitled to the same wisdom! Granted truth one, *I'm actually getting older*, is checked off the list, but maybe things haven't started to suck that badly and maybe they're not living life to the fullest yet. Your job is to help facilitate not only their comfort and your radius but their liberty and pursuit of happiness. So, no rushing the senior residence selection process.

The good news is that there are independent and government agencies that can help connect you with facilities for the folks. *A Place for Mom*, is one efficiently named not-for-profit agency that can do what its title suggests. The group also hosts a site to help find *A Place for Dad*. I can tell you with some authority that *A Place for Mom* makes good on the claim. Their eponymously named website states unequivocally that, "From finding the right care home, dementia care or assisted living facility to researching Veteran's benefits and financing senior care, we'll be with you each step of the way. All at no cost to you."

Another helpful website, http://www.usa.gov/Topics/Seniors.shtml also provides a lengthy list of resources courtesy of our tax dollars, so that's worth a peek as well.

Stage 5 – Carry On, My Wayward Mom

Okay, it's happened; the folks need help and there's no putting it off. Independent care is losing its "independence." Assistance is now required in areas like bathing, dressing, food preparation, etc. I don't know about you, but, while I'd be happy to whip up a stack of easily re-heated meals, bathing my parents would scar me in ways that would enrich therapists for years to come. Holding my naked stepfather aloft in a shower as I sluice the suds off of his pendulous scrotum with luke-warm water wouldn't just gross me out; it would give me PTSD. Just writing that will require some therapy.

If your circumstances are such that you and/or yours must step up and tend to your forebears, then you need to do some serious radius control! The housing and care of aging parents is a big deal. You should only have to get very old once, so enduring the rigors of your parent's process, then having to do it yourself a few rapidly approaching years later, is a fucking from life that must be avoided. Don't play this situation by ear; plan it carefully. Where will they stay? When will they eat? What time should the gifted drug mule puke up the sleeping pill? Also, how will the work be distributed? Leaving these questions unanswered will be your undoing.

Then there's your "you" time. You're already fucked up from your midlife crisis and struggling to create some personal space to get your personal thing on. Assuming you're not amoral or a sociopath, your feelings for you parents will be your best guide as you move through this difficult period. But when we "assume" we make an "ass" out of "ume" or something like that, so maybe your conscience isn't your best guide. Maybe you need an actual guide. The blurb for the book "How to Care for Your Aging Parents," actually reads, "When love is not enough—and, regrettably, it never is—this is an essential guide." Oprah digs it and it won the Books for a Better Life award. Even the Family Care Alliance called it an "excellent resource," Not only does it have wisdom from an assumed high school graduate, it also has templates that make organizing your parents' various pills, appointments and new "freckles," easy.

Chapter 7

THE WORLD

"The world owes you nothing. It was here first."

Mark Twain

Interpersonal interactions don't stop just because we leave those environments most familiar to us. We can find enough obstructions, direct confrontations and human children to annoy us anywhere in the world (though no children on the planet are as annoying as our homegrown stock, *U-S-A, U-S-A!*). We are all of us interconnected. I don't mean that in the *flick your cigarette in the gutter and it will eventually travel to the ocean and kill a fish* sort of way. I mean it in a more immediate *talk during the movie and give me a look when I ask you to keep it down,* or the *notice tourists in a beautiful place and offer to take their picture* kind of way. The world is certainly not getting any more polite, so maintaining a circumstance conducive to happiness is only getting harder. But given the MIDMEN credo…

1. I'm actually getting old.
2. It's ultimately going to suck.
3. Tough shit. I will still need to live life to the fullest until I can't anymore.

…we have to make the world work for us.

As we established earlier, you can be a dick sometimes, yes? This is not the best aspect of our personalities to put forward when it comes to making the world our bitch. Quite the opposite. Of course there will be times when we are legitimately wronged and have to pull some Mr. Hyde out of our Dr. Jekyll asses, but only as a last resort. Real control of our world radius requires that we think of others' radiuses as being as important as our own. A classic example would be if you're very tall and attending a standing room only event like a parade or a concert.

Someone aware that other radiuses exist in the same small space as their own wouldn't stand in the front. I know that's a "no duh" example, but it's amazing how many big, tall fuckheads don't consider it. The tall guy up front is only considering himself and that is evidence of an attitude that is unlikely to make him any new friends.

Based on my belief that material wealth beyond providing the essentials is inconsequential to one's happiness, I have no reason to treat those of influence better than those presumably without any. The owner of a restaurant is shown no more deference by me than the busboy. We're all equal until proven otherwise.

Protecting our radiuses by protecting the radiuses of others is a solid theory as long as everyone else is practicing the same method. But pretty much *no one* is. Not everyone is the tall douche in the front row, but not everyone is the Good Samaritan, either. Sadly, far too many people seem to be wandering through life glassy-eyed and interaction-free save their attachment to their Smartphone umbilical, or *Earbudical*™. Much like the description of karma earlier, controlling your surroundings can be viewed as a selfish act. Here again, by behaving in a certain way you are proving unequivocally that such behavior can be found right there at the center of your radius, because it's you. There are also numerous benefits. Politeness, friendliness and, if you have the skill, a decent joke can knock down all kinds of walls and open a world where people want to help you because they like you. Again, some, probably even most, won't be particularly beguiled by your charms, but a percentage totally will.

An honest assessment of our time and how we spend it will also relieve a great deal of world radius stress from our lives. The value we attribute to our time may just be the prime driver of stress in the course of our day. Here's a simple example. When I get home after a day out, I just want to sit in front of the TV and veg for a while. Unwind. So, to get that decompression started as soon as possible, I drive like a maniac to get home quickly. If some troglodyte is determined to drive in the passing lane without actually passing, I will tear the sky open with my great blaring horn. Why? So I can commence my precious sitting passively thing five minutes sooner. Conversely, if you're getting your MIDTWAT in a knot because you're late for an appointment, you could have controlled your time radius by leaving for it five minutes earlier! How easy is that?

Five minutes is five minutes and how we choose to value a given period of five minutes can make a significant difference in how we navigate our world. This is a lesson I still have some trouble embracing. I know that if I drive 75 instead of 65 for ten miles I will only save 1:14, so it can't possibly be the literal use of "time" chafing my hide. So I considered what it was that was pissing me off so bad about those who would dare slow my travels, whether on the freeway or in front of me on a movie ticket line, and it came down to radius control! The people who are pissing me off are doing so because they do not comprehend or respect that if I wish to pass on the freeway, the fast lane is *my* radius! I'm late for sitting on my ass in front of the TV for fuck's sake; I'm following the rules and paying attention to traffic. If the assholes in front of me aren't on the ball, they're not playing by the rules! I am justified in my tension, no? Yeah, sure, but who wins? As we've discussed, for me to try and exert my control by being a dick, I have to endure my own being of a dick. An added benefit to being aware of our own dickliness is that it automatically offers us insight into the dickliness of others. We know why the other guy is freaking out because we're not passing in the passing lane, etc.

The trick to not getting twisted when we're just trying to get from point A to point B, whether we're on the road, on line at the supermarket, or traversing a foreign land is simple: downgrade the value of our time. By overvaluing our time, we force ourselves to react to powers that for the most part don't even know we're alive. My approach to devaluing my own time has been to remove virtually all value from my time when it is in the hands of an uncaring society. I now appraise my time as being as worthless as shit. Think about it; how can someone waste my time when my time *is* waste? Someone wants into the lane? I'm the guy that lets them in. I also try to be aware that the reasons other people are erupting like stress-spewing volcanoes may be totally legitimate and unknown to me. If someone's wife is in the backseat of their speeding vehicle bellowing with the final throes of labor, I'm not sure my flipping off the driver is going to make things any easier. That old guy plodding along in front of me likely knows something I don't; time will pass no matter where I'm spending it. This is old guy wisdom that comes from knowing the clock is ceaselessly ticking on our lives, and explains why the people with the least time seem to have the most time.

Hey, I have one of my pithy little stories for this! I was recently told about a person who worked in the corporate world in New York City. She's a woman, but married to a MIDMAN so I have deemed her worthy and opened the literary velvet ropes of this book to allow her through. On the particular day on which this particular story takes place, her corporate job focused largely on enforcing rejection on decent, hopeful and often deserving people. It didn't make her feel good. At day's end she walked through the building following the path of heartbreak she herself had paved. She walked through the atrium lobby and out the big, fancy front door. Drawing a deep breath she d-zouble d-zutched herself into the Pamplona-like running of the suits that is the Madison Avenue sidewalk. Several blocks passed before she could peel herself away from the stampeding – if expensively scented – herd and dodge her way down the subway stairs. The train arrived quickly but, clearly having gotten the *cruel world* memo that was circulating on our businesswoman, offered no seating. All she wanted to do was sit quietly and run through some fucking papers. Fucking one of those fucking days.

As she stood by her selected pole, her tense shoulders hunching toward her ears, her upper lip tightening into a suggestion of a sneer, the doors opened at a stop and people got off, people got on; same ol', same ol'. But one guy, this one guy, all but skipped into the car happily. This fucking idiot had the balls to just look around at everyone and smile! What the fuck was this guy on? Next thing you know he's striking up conversations. . . with people who were smiling with him. Businesswoman glared at this freak with loathing and contempt. It's a cruel world and you can't just get all Jiminy Cricket and happy-go-lucky about it!

And then it hit her; the happy freak was someone she herself had rejected not two hours earlier! She ruined his life and yet here he was with his life clearly unruined. She thought back and replayed the meeting in her mind. His reaction to her rejection hadn't actually been too severe. Of course she assumed he was just being brave and stoic, but no, he just wasn't taking the beating. The epiphany was strong and forceful; he was controlling the radius of his environment. Not only was he creating the world he wanted to be in, others around him were interested in visiting that planet. She wanted to talk to him, tell him she was so happy to see that she hadn't crushed him and thank him for the valuable lesson he was teaching her there on the subway, but she was a coward and slipped out at the next stop before he could see her. Why harsh his buzz? But that was several years ago and the lesson has never left her. She enjoys people more now. She even enjoys *rejecting* people more now.

Chapter 8

THE MONEY

"All money makes possible is for you to stop worrying about money."

Paul Stanley of KISS

Reliable, common sense, standby Buddha said, "Desire is the root of all suffering." All too often we conflate our general well-being with how well we have satisfied our material desires. For instance, we assume that rich people are successful and less rich people are less so. We assume that a guy with a sexy wife is better satisfied physically, or that someone with an Aston Martin DB9 is more pleased to be driving. These are just assumptions and could easily be complete and total bullshit, except for the driving the DB9 part. This is not to say that a guy with a sexy woman next to him in his amazing car isn't happy; he very well may be, but having those things is far from a guarantee. Maybe she's paid for but the car isn't. Maybe the people with those amazing cars have to endure incredibly stressful circumstances to maintain their lifestyles. Or the men have to endure the pressure of providing their women with repeated, lengthy sessions of physical pleasure; dimming lights, slowly slipping them out of some sheer little something, making suggestive jokes as they sip a glass of cool white wine . . . the cost of which can really add up to . . . virtually nothing! You didn't expect that, did you? That guy could be you! Within reason, of course.

The pervasive goal of this book is to separate what really matters to us in our lives from what doesn't. This makes the subject of money and our relationship to it a very important area to examine. Wealth inequality in the USA is at its widest since 1920. I live in the Los Angeles area. The spectrum of personal wealth here is probably about as wide as it is anywhere. But interestingly, the people in my middle class, blue-collar suburban neighborhood are by all standards of measurement far happier than the people I encounter in Beverly Hills. The city where I live was ranked as 5th happiest in the USA last year. Beverly

Hills wasn't on the list. The most obvious standard by which we can judge public contentment is people's driving habits. A Honda CR-V in this city is about a million times more likely to let you into traffic than that Aston Martin in Beverly Hills.

If I had to distill the reasons for wealth-based assholiness down to a single cause, I would have to say it's a mentality issue. Getting wealthy (as opposed to having your money handed to you, after which you might still be an asshole, but the reasons would be different) generally requires a certain mindset. Most industries provide a great deal of competition and even if there's none, the free market itself is precarious to navigate. Like cops who become jaded and only view society as a bunch of losers just waiting to commit a crime, people seeking wealth can start viewing every aspect of their lives as competitive. So, a "your widget isn't going to displace my widget in the widget emporiums" mentality expands into "that eight feet of moving macadam in front of my car is mine and I will fucking kill you if you try to take it." Competition becomes a full time MO.

Meanwhile, not having enough money can also cause one to be what sociologists now call "Douchenozzle-enabled." This was a theory explored by Dr. Constantine Douchenozzle. What Douchenozzle's probing revealed was that redefining "need" created an improvement in attitude far more easily than an increase in personal wealth. This would suggest that if one is acting like an ass hat (no offense meant to the brilliant Cranial Proctologist, Dr. Gilmore Asshat), it certainly could be that they don't have the means to get what they need—but it also might mean that they have no idea what "need" really means.

The concept of too little or too much money has been explored scientifically and the findings revealed that you and I don't have enough money. Actually I do and you may too because the intersection between wealth and happiness may not be as expensive as you think. The Marist Institute for Public Opinion conducted a poll in 2012 that revealed big differences in contentment between people making $50K or more and people making less. The actual "golden" number was $67K; any more than that and no increased contentment was recorded. So if you're making $50-67K and you're miserable, don't blame money. However, if you don't have the money for rent or mortgage or the food to put on the table, it could make you pretty unhappy. If bills for things like lavish dining or a car you can't really afford are crunching you, then your attitude is the result of a poor assessment of what your genuine needs are. In either event, determining what we *need* and managing the acquisition of those things is key to creating an environment for discovering and exploiting what truly matters to us, which is the task at hand.

Earlier in the book you took a quiz to determine your desire in life and a little later you took another to establish the challenges facing you in its pursuit. Flip back to those for a moment and review your responses (I know you didn't write them in but I've been with you this whole book and you haven't changed a bit).

You will once again notice that there is no listing in the desire quiz for things like luxury cars. That is because they are ultimately bullshit. As I wrote, we cannot "car, cash or girl" our way out of our midlife crisis and those things sure as hell won't make paying our bills any easier! We need the time and presence of mind to suss our way through the greatest self-appraisal crisis of our lives; shitty financial conditions aren't going to make that any easier. And if our priorities are misdirected on top of that, we are in a perfect storm of bullshit. The main thrust of my cure for midlife crisis is the understanding of what matters in one's life and the pursuit thereof. If we set the bar of what matters artificially, we will never get a clear look at the real things.

That said, some material things do matter and where we stand in our money thing has a great influence on our overall sense of well-being. Okay, not according to the serene and holy Hindu sadhus I encountered in Varanasi, India who eschew all physical possessions, but fuck them. You *can* have too little money for all kinds of things: child support, traffic fines, food, credit card payment, "making it rain" or any combination of those things. If your problems are financial then you are unlikely to suddenly have the means to buy your way out of them, so an alternative resolution must be sought.

These can be very tough times. Many people have lost their jobs or their homes and are tight on cash. I won't make jokes at their expense because the last thing they need is another *expense*, ladies and gentlemen. Is this book on? Demographically, the modern MIDMAN is in a very tenuous spot with regard to financial stability. For many of us the market downturn in '08 wiped out a great deal of savings or pension and getting a new job is more challenging for the American MIDMAN than for almost all the other demos. CNN.com cites an Urban Institute study that found workers in their 50s to be about 20% less likely than workers ages 25 to 34 to become re-employed. Older workers also have the longest bouts of unemployment. The average duration of unemployment for workers ages 55 to 64 was 11 months as recently as January 2013, according to the Labor Department. That's three months longer than the average for 25 to 36-year-olds. What's saddest about this is that during the boom in which we were babied, the unemployment rate for people 65 and over was called *RETIREMENT*!

Unlike younger people, we have less time to recover our losses before reaching the time of life when we had planned to start digging into our savings. Many of us Baby Boomers, the oldest of whom are now of alleged retirement age, have been forced to postpone it. Kids in their 20s who normally would have moved out to start their own lives have been forced to stay at home or come back . . . and borrow their parents' retirement money.

Then there's the housing market. Many of us had the better part of our net worth wrapped up in our homes. When the prices took a shit, we lost much of our wealth. Or we may have gotten caught up in the mortgage debacle and now the house payments are upside down and we're facing foreclosure.

The listings below offer an overview of possible solutions to the more general 'changeable' money problems. If you are rich that's cool; you can read this chapter and say stuff like, "Yeah, that's what they need to do, damnable spendthrifts! *Roscoe*?! Where's my gimlet?"

Are you in debt? Even if the money has dried up, we want to continue living in the manner to which we become accustomed. Most of us turn to borrowing, though a desperate few will turn to prostitution. Sadly, the MIDMANWHORE market is a little soft, if you catch my meaning.

Fifty-five percent of American consumers are carrying credit card balances of eight to ten thousand dollars. According to Experion.com, the average total debt among Baby Boomers in 2012 was $101,951 and, because they're so cool, it's even higher for Gen X at $111,121.88.

Debt is a good example of the unfortunate facts of our lives that make it so much harder to stand down our midlife crises. We have the rapid passage of time, mortality and the mortifying shrinkage of our testes swirling around our heads already; calls from collection agencies aren't what I'd call a tonic. For you to get to that rarely visited place in your brain where it's peaceful enough for you to get anything that matters going, extraneous problems like debt must be confronted. Maintaining some manner of lifestyle while confronting debt is a Wallenda-sized balancing act. I've boiled it down to two steps:

1. Budget. I know people. A lot of people. Many of those people don't have a fucking clue when it comes to money. Some of them have the good fortune of earning enough to insulate themselves from their own fiduciary ignorance, but they're still headed for a personal market crash. Let's go back to the holy trinity:

1. I'm actually getting old.
2. It's ultimately going to suck.
3. Tough shit. I will still need to live life to the fullest until I can't anymore.

All three of these cost money. The level of suckage in item #2 is almost entirely dependent on the depth of our pockets. We're going to need to have some "Oh fuck!" money. While the proper care and feeding of your resources shouldn't be reliant on the sparse information herein, you may find a few valid jumping off points.

Spending money can be likened to running electrical power in your home. When all the lights and the TV are on, the meter outside is spinning like a Colgems' Monkeys 45 (spinning meters gone, records gone—one sentence, two arcane references, sweet). The idea is to keep life inside the house operating the way you like while keeping the meter spinning as slowly as possible. In the analogy, we would maintain our lifestyle but slow the meter's rotation by turning off lights and TVs in rooms we're not using, run the AC at a slightly higher temperature or run appliances at night when electrical rates are lower. And here the analogy and that which is being analogized meet; those very same actions would save money. Slowing the meter helps save money both literally and analgesically. Yes, I know that's pain medication; you hurt less when you're not worrying about money.

Unless we're bringing in Koch brothers, Bill Gates, or Taylor Swift money, we would be well-advised to spend conscientiously. But, since we're dedicated to reaping the most pleasure from our dwindling years, we need to figure out how to have it all. The cold acceptance of reality, present and likely future, is of the utmost importance. Understanding what we're bringing in and what we're shelling out tells us what we have to put away and what we can piss away. The Bank of America's Bettermoneyhabits.com has a slew of easy to watch videos on all this budget and debt stuff. They're like *Personal Finance for Dummies*; easy, clear and short. Or, you can always get *Personal Finance for Dummies*, which actually exists. If you head over here, https://www.bankofamerica.com/deposits/manage/creating-a-budget.go, you can get great advice and even download spreadsheets for your budgeting. If you're not doing this shit, you have got to do this shit. People wind up living in very difficult circumstances on measly government checks. These are people just like us who didn't get with it and anticipate their likely destiny. If you have money and debt and income, you're in a very good position not only to get old, but to have it suck less; of course the dead part is still the same.

2. Deal with it. The rules on dealing with debt when you have no money are actually fairly simple. They must be, the Federal Trade Commission was actually able to write a website on the subject! You can visit the site here, http://www.ftc.gov/bcp/edu/microsites/money-matters/dealing-with-debt.shtml but I'll hip you to a few cautionary nuggets:

a) Debt Collection. As I said, nobody wants to hear from a collection agency. If you had the money you'd pay the debt (you would, right?). If you're behind in paying your bills, you can expect to hear from a debt collector. A debt collector is more often than not someone other than the creditor who regularly collects debts owed to someone else. Lawyers can also be debt collectors. Okay, read my lips, or rather, read my writing: by federal law, collection agencies MUST STOP CONTACTING YOU IF YOU REQUEST IT IN WRITING. I shit you not. It's that easy. If you've been getting harassed by a collection agency you fucking owe me big time, Jack. (Yeah, um, one thing; they *can* contact you to tell you they're suing you, they just can't ask you for money anymore.)

b) Debt Relief Services. You may think that a company that promises to erase the debt for pennies on the dollar is the answer to your prayers. Not true! Don't use them. They don't have magical powers.

What debt relief services are *suggesting* is that by hiring them you will have access to their superior connections and know-how, and that they will lower your debt without your having to actually pay 100% of it. Nonsense. What they will likely do is charge you 15% of your debt up front and then discuss lowering your future interest rates with your various creditors, then collect a little somethin' somethin' every month as they distribute your money to your creditors for you. Fuck that. You can do both of those things and save yourself the 15% upfront and the vig.

The United States Government Accountability Office put out a report on this very subject called "Debt Settlement: Fraudulent, Abusive, and Deceptive Practices Pose a Risk to Consumers." I'm not sure why I suddenly trust the US Government to tell me who not to trust, but the book says the majority of the for-profit companies in the debt settlement racket use "fraudulent, deceptive, and abusive practices." Hiring the wrong one could provide you with exactly the opposite of your desired result.

c) Credit Repair. Every day, companies target people who have poor credit histories with promises to clean up their credit reports so they can get a car loan, a home mortgage, insurance, or even a job – after paying a fee for the service. The truth is that no one can remove accurate negative information from your credit report. It's illegal.

Here is what the Federal Trade Commission has to say about credit repair companies (I lifted it from their site verbatim because I am a fucking tax payer and my fucking tax dollars built that fucking site):

"You see the ads in newspapers, on TV, and online. You hear them on the radio. You get fliers in the mail, email messages, and maybe even calls offering credit repair services. They all make the same claims:

"Credit problems? No problem!"

"We can remove bankruptcies, judgments, liens, and bad loans from your credit file forever!"

"We can erase your bad credit — 100% guaranteed."

"Create a new credit identity — legally."

Do yourself a favor and save some money, too. Don't believe these claims: they're very likely signs of a scam. Indeed, attorneys at the Federal Trade Commission, the nation's consumer protection agency, say they've never seen a legitimate credit repair operation making those claims. The fact is there's no quick fix for creditworthiness. You can improve your credit report legitimately, but it takes time, a conscious effort, and sticking to a personal debt repayment plan."

The National Foundation for Credit Counseling can be reached at 800-388-2227 or http://www.nfcc.org/. They'll put you together with the NFCC Member Agency closest to you. It's not free, but it is low cost and as I understand it, you won't get ripped off.

d) Advance Fee Loans. If you're looking for a loan or credit card but don't think you'll qualify – or if you've been turned down by a bank because of your credit history – you may be tempted by ads and websites that guarantee loans or credit cards, regardless of your credit history. Should you apply, you'll likely find out that you have to pay a fee just for the promise of the loan. Best to ignore these ads or sites.

If you have to pay a fee for the promise of a loan or credit card, you're dealing with a scam artist. More than likely, you'll get just an application for a credit card, a stored value or debit card, or a card that has so many strings attached it qualifies as a Macy's Thanksgiving Day Parade balloon.

e) Pre-Paid Cards. Okay, there's actually something to these, though caution must be exercised. Let's say you were given credit at a time in your life when you simply shouldn't have been (yes, in this example you're me in my late teens and Macy's had the most liberal card qualifications AND the only Ticketron machine in town). So you max the card or cards, miss multiple payments, and to this day your credit is shit. You live in the 21st century so you actually require a credit card to get anything done. Pre-paid cards are not used to help rebuild your credit. There are other methods for that that I'll hit in a moment, but a pre-paid card can solve a lot of other banking problems.

Banks have gotten more and more guarded about offering services, from loans all the way down to simple savings/checking accounts. This may come as a shock to the MIDMAN as we can easily recall a time when they would not only open an account for you; they would celebrate the act by giving you a toaster. Banks reject business from people they deem to be one of the "underbanked." According to CreditCardInsider.com, the underbanked are people who "do not have standard access to mainstream financial institutions, and who must rely instead on check-cashing facilities and non-traditional providers." According to the Federal Deposit Insurance Corporation (FDIC), there are about 24 million of you out there.

There are several cards on the market that offer you a prepaid solution. I am only going to discuss one because it seems to have the most versatility and affordability so it can lend you some tranquility to provide midlife mobility (I hope you were human beatboxing there). Bluebird by American Express seems to have it all going on. The card is a team effort from American Express and Wal-Mart so you should be able to find an outlet nearby. It offers you no credit; you fund what you're expecting to spend, but it does offer things like deposits by Smartphone, mobile bill pay, no minimum balance, ATMs, the elusive checking account and no account maintenance fees. Pretty much everything you get from an American Express card, from consumer protection to 24/7 telephone servicing, is included with this card. There are other cards, like the Green Dot Card or The Approved Card from Suze Orman, which may well be a better fit for you than this one. I will say that the 30 minutes I put into research (don't worry, my compensation was included in the price of this book) put the Bluebird on top. You'll need to do some homework, but do so knowing there is a cost-effective way for you to be carrying a valid credit card that is tantamount to legal tender for all debts public and private.

f) Vehicle Repossession. If you're like most people, you rely on your vehicle to get you where you need to go when you need to go, whether it's to work, the grocery store, or on the lam. But if you're late with your car payments, or in some states, if you don't have adequate auto insurance, your vehicle could be taken away from you. Again, this is just an overview, but basically when you purchased or leased your car you put the company with which you did business in the catbird seat. If you don't make your payments on time they can repossess the thing. They can also sell it to another company who could repossess it and sell it again! They actually have to tell you where they're selling it and for how much so you can try to buy it back, which makes zero sense since you already had it and couldn't afford it.

The next item will delve more deeply into this, but much like the broken record that is the bulk of this book; honesty and transparency are your best friends here. If you're going to be late with a payment get on the blower and talk to your creditor. Their situations will vary so some may feel that working it out with you is easier than repossession and some may differ. You'll never know which one you have if you don't try. There are a wide variety of rules and regulations within these circumstances nationally, and even more when you parse them locally so I will do what great advisors have done since time immemorial and pass the buck. Go here: http://www.consumer.ftc.gov/articles/0144-vehicle-repossession

g) Negotiating with Credit Card Companies. (To be delivered like Jackie Gleason saying, "Miami Beach audiences are the greatest audiences in the world!" assuming you're deep boomer enough to know what that means.) Credit card debt is the worst kind type of debt in the world! And *aawwaaay* we go!

According to a CNN Money article, there are two kinds of debt: good debt and bad debt. "Good" means you needed cash for stuff you couldn't afford, you had the income to pay it back, and you didn't want to dig into your savings or investments to get the cash. Bad debt is the loan you took out to buy that Aston Martin DB9 while earning a Nissan Versa salary.

According to CreditCards.com, the worst form of debt is credit cards. The site claims that in 2012, the average U.S. household with at least one credit card carried a credit card balance of around

$15,950! Jeez, a brand new Nissan Versa is only $12,000! Not coincidentally, personal bankruptcies are at all-time highs.

If you're carrying credit card debt you can't handle, there are a couple of things you can do. The first is; if at all possible, stop using your credit card. Only spending actual cash will give you that wonderfully tactile feeling of your resources slipping through your fingers like green water from corroded copper pipes. The second is this old chestnut: get honest. Figure out your budget based on your actual income and not on your *who-cares-I'm-fucked-anyway* depression or *everything-works-out-fine-in-the-end* delusional optimism. There are other books that specialize in putting together these kinds of plans, so ask your wife to buy one for you. But for the time being, let's assume that the budget you create allows for some small amount of money to be dedicated to credit card payments. If you only carry debt with one company, then the next step is easy: call that bank and have a conversation about what you can afford and how some of the pressures can be taken off of you. For instance, most credit card companies will not only accept considerably smaller payments—you know, if they actually receive them—but they will also stop compounding the interest. That's a pretty huge thing when you consider that Premier Bankcard, the South Dakota credit card marketer, actually tested a card with 79.9% annual percentage rates (APRs)! Wait, here's the kicker; the cards only had a $300 credit limit. Okay, that may seem nuts but it's actually pretty standard for a card to collect an all-time high average interest rate of 14.78%! Your friendly neighborhood Mafia loan shark would only stick you with 6-10% per week compounded weekly.

If you owe money to various institutions (meaning banks; the Harrah's Resort and Casino is not an "institution" by these terms) then there actually may be agencies that can assist you! These are known as debt consolidation agencies. According to Wikipedia (which means I could have written this myself and posted it there – but I didn't), "Debt consolidation entails taking out one loan to pay off many others. This is often done to secure a lower interest rate, secure a fixed interest rate or for the convenience of servicing only one loan." Generally you're going to need some kind of collateral to pull this off, like, oh, I don't know, *YOUR HOME!* The thing to remember is that lending institutions don't really want you to go bankrupt (see next item) because then they don't get shit. However, or should I say, HOWEVER, you can't just assume this technique will save your financial ass. There are unscrupulous debt consolidation companies and there is always the son of a bitch who got you into this trouble in the first place: you! Once you start getting your credit back you have to change your spending behavior or you'll just screw the pooch anew. Again, this isn't specifically a book of financial advice; in fact, I'm getting bored shitless with this topic so allow me to point you in the direction of a great article you can find online about debt consolidation: http://money.usnews.com/money/blogs/my-money/2013/04/12/4-debt-consolidation-traps-to-avoid You'll still have a lot of homework to do, but this guy puts it in great terms.

h) Filing for Bankruptcy. Simple; you file for bankruptcy and all of your debts are forgiven and your credit is fucked for seven years. Use the techniques above to avoid this at all costs.

Do you hate your job? Another money problem MIDMEN frequently confront has nothing to do with debt or even unemployment. They have jobs. They just fucking hate them! Here's a really daunting statistic; a recent Gallup poll revealed that 70% of Americans polled either hate their jobs or are "disengaged" from their work. Obviously, that puts the odds of actually enjoying your job way against you. If you're in the

30% who goes to work without complaint, nice! One more obstacle to your clarity and self-discovery has been removed. But if you're among the 70% of Americans who hate their jobs, consider this: it's only part of your life. As I have been chanting like a monk with OCD throughout this book, the game here is to accept the problems inherent in being alive in western society (I specify western because this difference in opportunity and access to resources is totally different in developing societies) and sort them out to the extent that you can identify and follow your dreams, yes? So viewing a job as only one aspect of your life, and arguably not the most important aspect, could be necessary to achieve that goal. The luxury of filling your days doing what you love is not afforded everyone. That's just a fact. But we can make a choice; we can either change jobs if that's possible (it may not be), or we can put the unfortunate situation in some kind of proper perspective and accept that we will be getting our quality of life experiences elsewhere.

If you're in a job you should keep but are unhappy with it, there are a few general ways to manage. First and foremost, prioritize the job. Being a charming raconteur will certainly keep you from lunching alone, but nothing enlarges your work balls like getting the job done right. Being conscientious about your work and legitimate in your dealings will keep you operating at a very desirable level for your employer. If you're the proprietor, your professionalism and legitimacy will place you in a position to expect the same from your people. If you work alone, like one of those guys whose job it is to sit in a nuclear missile silo playing solitaire until there's a call to release the big one (do your own fart joke), you don't really have these problems.

At work, most of us must not only interact with other people, some of whom may hold positions of authority and needn't endure our bullshit, but also negotiate our way through our designated tasks. This often creates interpersonal challenges, or worse, friendships. The more we like someone the harder it is to tell them we're too busy to kibitz (that's *shoot the shit* for my goyisha brothas). If we don't like someone, we treasure the ability to say (as Bill Lumberg *of Office Space*), "Yeah, yeah, um listen if I could just kind of do this stuff here, that would be terrific, OK? Great."

I have a nice technique for stopping instant messaging conversations. We all have people in our lives who don't understand when a texting communication is over. We don't want to "hang up" on them but if the fucking phone vibrates again, we're going to freak out. It's so easy to end these things you won't believe it: the smiley face emoticon. The smiley face emoticon is essentially the digital communication version of calling a bet in poker. Your texter sees the smiley face emoticon and thinks, "Do I want to text again and raise, or should I go out?" They better have something pretty fucking good in that hand to talk about before they go all in after a smiley face. Nine times out of ten, they fold.

But no matter how you have to secure the area to get your job done, do it and get the job done. This is a positive all the way around. As the ancient Romans used to say, *labor omnia vincit*, which translates to *hard work conquers all*, which they proved by working hard and conquering all.

My favorite way for MIDMEN to insulate themselves from a job they hate is by faking a handicap. Deaf/mute would be my recommended physical challenge. What could be better? You can't hear them and they didn't want to hear you in the first place. But seriously, the best defense in almost every workplace situation is a good offense, so be offensive. How can you make yourself impervious or at least resistant to the abuses of a despised workplace? Two rules:

1. <u>Rule one: Never bitch</u>. No complaining, no matter how justified. If asked about the circumstance or condition of anything, including your physical being, the answer should be something in the area of, "No complaints." As a

small business employer I can tell you from personal experience that complainers inspire others to complain and cause discontent among a staff. Employers view them as a morale and productivity cancer and remove them as quickly as possible. Even if the offending bitch pitcher hasn't done enough damage to be fired, he'll still be the first to go if there are cutbacks. "Fuck that guy; he's always complaining" is much easier to say than, "Gosh, Billy's a great guy but we're going to have to let him go."

2. Rule two: Kick ass. Being 100% competent is the best offense and defense you have in your work environment. You may be surrounded by saboteurs, scoundrels and rogues (that's right, in this example you work on a pirate ship) but when push comes to shove, being on your game will put you on the right side of every situation. Your boss will respect and appreciate you, your co-workers will see the obvious respect your boss has for you, and you will be able to take or reject whatever liberties you'd like. By that I mean you could ask for time off and get it from your boss, or tell your co-workers you're too busy to do XYZ. Employees are like voters; they don't understand the power their actions actually have.

But keeping your head down and getting your shit done can be challenged by certain unforeseen, um, challenges:

Young Twerp Boss? More MIDMEN are reporting to bosses younger then themselves every day. A 2010 survey by the jobs website CareerBuilder found that 43% of workers over 35 are reporting to a younger boss. The traditional *they're-too-young-to-know-they're-going-to-die* and *you're-aware-that-you're-doomed* generation gap has been all but usurped by the *technology* generation gap. Sure, there may be some nostalgic charm to the way we did it back in the day, but your boss doesn't give a shit. Get good at your Smartphone and/or any other modern gear you're going to need. Adapt to your boss's work process and excel (both the spreadsheet program and the actual act of excelling).

Here's a quick story. My friend Billy was an experienced insurance adjuster. That's the guy who shows up to assess damage and advise the insurance company on what the policy holder's settlement should be. He wears a trademark bow tie and permanent smile and fits right in with my friends, some of whom, you may recall, are magicians. Billy is vocationally perfect for the job of insurance adjuster as he has this great way of making people feel like everything will be all right. After years of working with the same team, his insurance company hired a new, young supervisor who assigned Billy an iPhone so that he could connect to the office by FaceTime while doing inspections. One of the things Billy loved about being in the field was not having anyone over his shoulder. He politely demurred on the FaceTiming, supporting his objection with a hilarious story about walking into the wrong mobile home while the residents were *in flagrante delicto* in cosplay wearing big fluffy animal costumes (he a pink bear and she a weird bird thing). His adolescent firebrand of a boss laughed heartily at the bawdy story, told Billy he understood his feelings and fired his ass on the spot. I told you it was a quick story. I neglected to tell you it was a lie fabricated for illustrative purposes.

Corporate Merger or the Marketplace Devaluates You? Cutbacks or myriad other reasons cause companies to let people go. Generally it's because someone incredibly rich is certain that another couple million in the bank will finally enlarge their dick to a tolerable size. But regardless of the reason, MIDMEN are on the front lines of cutbacks. According to *Newsweek* in an article called "The Beached

White Male," things can get pretty shitty for Daddy. They wrote, "The recession hit all sectors of the economy, but one demographic was dealt a blow from which it may never recover: college-educated, middle-aged white men. Part of why the layoffs have been so striking is that they're so unprecedented." You don't have to be college educated or white either, just middle aged.

NBCNews.com ran a great piece on surviving mergers a few years back. One important factor it pointed out is that the new boss or new and improved old boss (now with more stress!) doesn't want to have to reinvent the wheel. The people who are doing the best job, either according to the boss's own observations or the recommendation of a department manager, are going to be an asset. So the first rule is no sucking. In fact, take on more responsibility. Implicate yourself into projects that are generally outside your area if you can. If you have a more versatile scope of experience, you can be useful in more ways.

Another commonly made mistake is that worried employees at merging companies hunker down like little kids hiding under the covers from the boogieman. In this situation, you need to do exactly the opposite: get out of bed and meet the boogieman face-to-face. If there are new people coming into your company as the result of a merger, be curious about them. Now this doesn't mean wandering into their offices and coquettishly kicking your toes at the floor like Sniffles the Mouse while sing-songing, "Whatcha doin'?" If it's logical, ask for a short appointment to familiarize them or yourself or both of you about the others' gig. Chatting in common spaces is also smart.

Finding a Job? Let's just pull the book over onto the shoulder and drop it into neutral for a moment. I want to add up a pair of facts I've already addressed. Fact one: MIDMEN are the most frequently fired and least frequently re-hired. Fact two: we are given to depression. An article (okay, it was really more of a blurb) in a recent edition of the AARP Bulletin reported a new government study, which I assume means the US Government—I don't know how informative a report by the government of Djibouti is going to be to American retired people—revealed a 45% jump in suicides for men 54-64, and an even higher 48% rise for men specifically in their 50s. A *Wall Street Journal* article reported that in "May 2013, the unemployment rate for people ages 45 to 64 was 6%, some 10 points lower than for people under 25. But the lower rate disguises the fact that when middle-aged people lose their jobs, it's much harder for them to find a new one. Those between 45 and 64 take almost a year on average to find a job, more than two months longer than workers between 25 and 44." Finding a job is a possible solution to a very big problem and that problem is depression. So, as beaten down and apathetic as we might be, even rightfully, we must find it within ourselves to stage a forward life assault.

The suggestions offered in the different chapters of this guide do not necessarily work independently of one another. A job search is a good illustration. If the MIDMAN is setting out to get a job, the information in the surrounding chapters will make the information below much more valuable. Removing some tension from his home radius, exercising more, eating and sleeping better, and focusing some longer-term attention on his appearance, can't hurt his chances!

How does a MIDMAN get a job? This is no mean feat for the majority of us, but it is possible. I've already covered a couple of important bases to hit when re-entering the job market, those being attitude and an awareness of technology. Here are a couple of other great tips to help you restart or continue your resources-in/resources-out cycle.

Salary demands: You may well have experience and a resume that should demand a pretty nice salary. Unfortunately, the competition for the job you need is younger than you and, whether they think they deserve it or not, more than likely they haven't put in the time to demand big bucks. The employers, for their part, have less of a problem offering less money for more person. If you want the job, you may have to adjust your salary demands to make yourself competitive with the young upstarts in the marketplace. You may also have to consider changing your location. Younger workers have an edge here, too. They're less likely to have purchased a house or dug in their roots and are more likely to say, "Sure, dude, I'll totally move to Djibouti."

Government programs: There are several government programs to keep you working hard and fed during hard times, though according to my research none offers a better health care plan or easier admission than prison. That said, you may not be the group shower type, so let's explore some alternatives:

- **The Trade Adjustment Assistance program**: According to an online brochure that can be found here, http://www.doleta.gov/tradeact/pdf/2011_brochure.pdf, the Trade Adjustment Assistance (TAA) program is a "federal entitlement program that assists U.S. workers who have lost or may lose their jobs as a result of foreign trade. This program seeks to provide adversely affected workers with opportunities to obtain the skills, credentials, resources, and support necessary to become re-employed." To get in, you have to file a petition with the US Department of Labor either online or by snail mail. You also only have one year after your dismissal to file.
- **Investigate fields friendly to men your age**: In 2013, the AARP (just join already; who are you kidding) put together a list of the "Fifty Best Employers for Workers Over 50," which I assume would also be helpful for workers on the slightly younger side of 50. Here is the link to the list: http:/www.aarp.org/work/employee-benefits/best_employers/. Health care, government

and financial services were the fields with the greatest presence on the list. Not found on the list were jobs like: skateboard trick-doer, hair-grower for wigmakers, getter-upper from comfy chair to get that thing over there-er, silent sports viewer or MIDMANWHORE.

- **The AARP job board**: Getting my AARP card was a painful experience for me. I didn't know that it would come in the form of a convenient mental suppository, another cutting edge innovation from the brilliant Cranial Proctologist, Dr. Gilmore Asshat. My invitation to join arrived literally the day after my 50th birthday. If they're going to be that prompt, shouldn't they at least disguise it as a birthday card? I wrestled with whether to join, and pragmatism won out over ego resulting in my current membership. Notwithstanding a great lead on long-term care insurance and a couple of 10% discounts at hotels, the organization's real value has been in information delivery. The newsletters, the magazines, and the website are all chock-full of great tidbits for the man on the slower go. This is a great example. You can find the AARP jobs board at http://www.aarp.org/jobs. I just did a search for copywriter jobs and 20 came up, all of which could be done from anywhere. Your specific skill or desired gig may require geographical proximity, but this is still a resource worth trying.
- **Teaching English as a Foreign Language (TEFL)**: This suggestion will probably strike you as the best suggestion in the world or the worst. It requires an adventurous spirit, some homeschooling, and a passport. There are jobs all over the world for Americans who would like to teach English. There's TEFL and TESL, Teaching English as a Second Language, and of course there's SOL, which is Shit Outta Luck, meaning you ain't leaving that comfy chair if you ain't working.

> Several online courses can be found with a simple search, and cost less than $500. I actually got mine for $65 with a Groupon! Then I dropped out. GED men are born, not made. The courses take from 40 to 120 hours depending on the level of diploma you want. Once you're armed with your TEFL cert, you can start job hunting online as well. *Teaching House* is a nice clearinghouse for keeping you living *in* a house: http://www.teachinghouse.com/english-teaching-jobs?gclid=CJrhquasnb0CFYtDMgodbEkAxw. If you possess that magical combination of wanderlust and desperation and would consider picking up a TEFL cert, you could work all over the damn world!

Money is a necessity if we want to survive in this crazy world without actually learning wilderness survival skills. The accumulation of money can be tricky sometimes, but the argument that doing so is possible for anyone with enough pragmatism and initiative is an easy one to make. The real trick is to sort what you *want* from what you *need.* Remember the words of Paul Stanley that headed this chapter, *"All money makes possible is for you to stop worrying about money."* Or if you consider a man wearing whiteface and a black star on his eye untrustworthy, consider what Mick Jagger had to say on the subject, "You can't always get what you want but if you try sometime, you just might find, you get what you need." Or if you need a rock philosopher who takes himself more seriously, Bono nailed it, "You can never get enough of what you just don't need."

Chapter 9

THE MIND

"I play into the perception of me, but it's really not me."
Kim Kardashian

Just who the hell do you think you are? Do you ever consider the answer to that question or have you simply adapted yourself to what other people think you are? The *you* that you present to the world might not be the real you. A nice example might be an upstanding priest. He might constantly, as Jimmy Carter said, "lust in his heart," but the *him* he decided to be doesn't allow him to be the real him, who happens to be a horny guy with an uncomfortable collar. He has studied in the seminary, been awarded a parish and created a perception of himself for others that may not mesh with who he actually is. Now he must live as the guy everyone assumes he is and suppress much of his real self. Well, gentlemen, confession time; that priest in that example was me. Just kidding (Jewy roots, remember?).

Having people misperceive who we are is not the worst thing in the world in and of itself, but succumbing to that false identity might be. Shakespeare said, "To thine own self be true, and it must follow, as the night the day, thou canst not then be false to any man." As MIDMEN who grew up presumably in western civilization, we have spent much of our lives in a society that doesn't *vivre le difference* easily. Our world has been heavily peopled by the sexist, the racist, and the little noticed, bassist. Since we all possess an innate desire to belong, we will often adapt the positions of those around us. We sacrifice the real us in favor of a more acceptable us so that even if we're living a lie, we're popular. An example of this could be the guy who has no problem with black people but lives within a sphere of racists and gets positive reinforcement after telling a crude joke about them. It is much harder for thine to be true to thyself than it is to be accepted by your immediate crowd. Let's be honest, you're a quirky fuck and society does not make it easy for you to express that. The hilarious novelist, Christopher Moore, brilliantly and, as I will now prove, quotably said, "If you think anyone is sane you just don't know enough about them."

If you get any one thing out of this book it should be the satisfaction of knowing that I spent your purchase price on something cool. If you get two things out of it, the second should be that being yourself is, in and of itself, doing something that matters to you. If "yourself" happens to be a Bernie Maddoff or worse, a K.C. of the Sunshine Band variety, you may want to keep your worst traits unindulged, but you still have to acknowledge and serve them somehow.

I was at my goddaughter's fifth birthday party not long ago and met a guy who was the ultimate Renaissance man. The first surprising fact I learned about Ace (not his real name, but I really don't think he'd mind if it were) came a moment after my wife and I entered the party. On the kitchen island was the perfect birthday cake for a five-year-old princess-obsessed girl: a pink Cinderella birthday cake with an edible, ornate hoop skirt and a plastic princess doll torso sticking out of the top. This was "Cake Boss" level stuff. We assumed it was store bought, but no—Ace made it. He had signed his son up for a cake making class but when they arrived it turned out the kid was too young so Ace took the class anyway, brought the lessons home and taught the kid himself! He also could have built the kid a kitchen to bake his cakes in and a house to put the kitchen in because he's an accomplished DIYer! Oh, and a sheriff; Ace is unmistakably a sheriff. He looks like a cop: close-cropped hair, solid stocky build, clear direct stare, proximal phalange-splintering handshake. When we met he was training for marine duty; he would be supervising a police boat crew and had to learn the skills. He's also a musician and has formed a band with other officers. Among the many instruments he plays is the bugle, a skill he uses to play Taps at officers' funerals. He also practices martial arts. He also has a green thumb and can turn dirt into beauty and nutrition at his whim. He's also not afraid to do housework and, according to my goddaughter's mother, teaches volumes to the boys simply by letting them see his biceps flex as he folds a T-shirt. Ace's brother is in Denmark, gay and out. Ace stands with his brother even to the extent that he has alienated their homophobic father. My point is this: if Ace can be Ace, you being you can't be that hard.

One of the major challenges we face as we suffer the depression-provoking transmogrification from immortal to too mortal is maintaining or establishing a healthy level of self-approval. When we're young immortals, we don't consider that every moment we spend compromising is another moment we didn't live for ourselves. But when the Grim Reaper parks his bony ass at our door and puffs his cigarettes waiting for our final 30 or so years to speed by, how each remaining moment services our deeply felt needs matters!

Carl Jung said, "We overlook the essential fact that achievements which society rewards are often won at the cost of diminution of personality. Many aspects of life which we should have experienced lie in the lumber room of dusty memories." Understanding what matters to us requires that we balance not just our personal priorities and idealistic desires, but the impact our thoughts and actions have on us versus the world around us. There are some rightfully and wrongfully angry people among us. It doesn't matter if the reasons are political, religious, or just a reaction to events in our radius, the anger is just as destructive to our mental and even physical well-being. If you possess a deep, seething hatred for the President, for instance (and we all seem to get a turn at that), you are wasting yourself with it. You're wasting your time, your emotion, and compromising your physical health. According to the Better Health Channel, being constantly pissed off can cause, among other nasty things, headaches, digestive problems, depressions, high blood pressure and its ugly cousins heart attack and stroke.

If we can, just for a moment, disregard the arguably valid external reasons we're so fucking angry and consider what the internal reason might be, we may find that we're harboring resentment for any number of life's unfair slights and find that the President, or whatever, is just a straw man. The world is going to hell; we all get that. If we want to control our anger, we have to weigh our impact on the situation that bugs us. If all we're doing is watching our political news channel of choice (coughing into hand, "*MSNBC and FOX*") and bloviating about how unbelievably ill-informed the goons who watch the other channel are, then we're just going to explode. If we balance our anger at society with an understanding of the anger our personal lives have inspired and put that anger into action on both fronts, working for a cause and striving for some version of inner peace, we can diffuse the bomb within. You will not end world hunger. Bono couldn't do it, Angelina Jolie couldn't do it and you sure as hell can't do it. Not alone, anyway. But you can address your pent-up crazy by joining the fight. There is a great ad campaign from the Rainforest Alliance. It's demographically aimed directly at, well, people like me, but the message of doing *something* instead of *everything* or *nothing* is brilliantly made. You can view it here: http://vimeo.com/49805510. You're not going to save the world alone, and causing yourself a stroke freaking out about it helps no one, especially you!

So it is time to ask ourselves the musical question: am I living for myself? Have I been true to myself and it hasn't turned out the way I'd hoped? That's right, another quiz. Read the questions; answer honestly, blah, blah, blah.

THE "TO THINE OWN SELF BE TRUE… OR FALSE" TEST

Basically, what we're going to do here is read a series of sentences and rate whether we are more apt to approach it as we would wish to or as society (family, boss, a judge's orders, etc.) would have us handle it. Just check the box that comes closest to describing you.

	True	False
The clothes I'm wearing match my personal style.		
My job (assuming I have one) satisfies me.		
My significant other is a perfect match.		
I feel good about myself.		
My social plans are of my own choosing.		
I am my own man.		
I am honest with myself.		
I am happy.		
I am optimistic.		
I think I may be coming down with something.		

Like the other revelatory quizzes in this book, this one ain't tarot cards; you don't need a psychic to decipher the answers. The good news is there is only good news in the results of this test. Even if all your answers leaned on the "false" side of the page, you have just allowed yourself to see your situation clearly, maybe for the first time. What you are likely to have found is that your world is not entirely under your control. There are compromises you have to make, and some of them may not make you too happy. You may have found that in spite of it, you really like yourself, or think you still look pretty damn good. Obviously, the combinations are endless.

One great way to clarify who you are is to envision a catastrophe in your life. Consider how you would react to a worst-case scenario. Would you persevere? Collapse? Assuming you haven't already confronted a significant tragedy (if you have, I am truly sorry), honestly envisioning how you would react could reveal a great deal about who you are at your core.

This entire book is dedicated to one thing and one thing only: helping you identify and/or act upon what matters to you so you don't wig out and become another midlife suicide stat – or just a miserable old fuck. Okay, it's actually two things; there's the whole *'selling of books for profit'* part.

As we configure the brain to support our quest for what matters, we may have to tweak our thought patterns. We have conditioned our brains to accept truths that may not be so truthful. Here are a couple of common brainwashes we need to rinse out again:

I'm old. This one drives me fucking crazy. I am so sick of hearing guys my age or younger than me referring to themselves as old. Seriously, fuck that. You may look a bit older than you used to, you may have let yourself go physically, but if you died, people would be saying you died young. You're young. Saying you're old is an excuse to do less. While I'm writing this, William Shatner is running his 82-year-old ass all over creation . . . on a fucking horse! Sure, sometimes we'll get thoughts running through our heads that are different than the thoughts we had when we were younger. For instance, last night I was brushing my teeth and thought, "I still have all my teeth." That's not really something that runs through a 30-year-old's head unless he's an MMA fighter. But I NEVER think of myself as old, or at least not too old to do what I need to do to enjoy my life. I'll get into ways to feel and look younger physically in the next chapter, but this is about your mind.

A study published in the *Journal of Personality and Social Psychology* reported that self-esteem increases throughout our lives and peaks at age 60. This means that guys our age who are dealing with depression and self-loathing are the exceptions. We're supposed to be feeling all cool and shit, but we undermine ourselves.

One of the reasons we may call ourselves old is because age is associated with retirement and we think we're ready to stop. And wanting to stop might have something to do with not wanting to continue what we're currently doing because we don't like it. So, we're not actually old, we're simply uninspired. The easy argument is, "My back is out and I can't do anything," or "My knees are shot. Walking hurts so I just want to sit down." Sorry, but, bullshit. I had the opportunity to direct a troupe of actors in Cambodia. These people are as a poor as can be and live in the harshest of conditions, but they have a story to tell and they get themselves to the stage and get up there and tell that story. The story is that they have each been in a landmine accident. They've lost limbs or one or two of their senses, but they love to tell their story. (Plug; you can learn more about them at http://LandmineSurvivorsCambodia.com.)

I can't imagine one of my cushy little western problems stopping me from doing what I love to do. I *can*, however, easily imagine no more than an annoying splinter stopping me from doing something I *don't* want to do.

You're not old; you're just uninspired. Allow yourself to truly believe that you can indulge yourself in your choice of undertaking. Be bold. In 2010, Ellen Johnson Sirleaf, Liberia's president since 2006, gave the Harvard commencement speech and said this: "If your dreams do not scare you, they are not big enough." Men have felt this way about boobs for years, now we need to apply it to our dreams.

I feel unproductive. Hey, you may actually *be* unproductive, but that's not the only reason for feeling this way. You could be very productive as, say, a father. You could coach the little league team or be in the middle of helping your kid move or get married while holding down your job at the same time and still feel unproductive. You could be on vacation sitting in a beach chair next to an icy glass of something icy in a glass and still feel unproductive.

The reason we feel unproductive is not based on what our actual output is, but on how satisfied we are with the direction of that output. If we are constantly involved in activities that we don't consider rewarding and not doing for ourselves, we will always feel unproductive.

Or we may be perfectly productive by normal societal standards but can't seem to get that lovin' feeling from ourselves because we may have been erroneously called losers as kids, or correctly identified as losers as the case may be. This charge is more often than not based on our not having lived up to another's expectations, say a parent or teacher. Unfortunately, *Loser Conditioning* (good title for a sequel, no?) is a spiraling process that reinforces the "loser's" disbelief in himself over a period of years. For example, if your school grades weren't particularly good it might have been caused by a learning disorder, problems at home, or nothing more complicated than the curriculum being uninteresting. Your parents and teachers didn't like the low grades and thought that criticizing you harshly would improve them. You returned to the classroom embittered, more distracted, or just turned off, and your grades got suckier. Everyone continued to shove the fact that you sucked at getting decent grades in your face and you became rebellious. This kind of juvenile rebelliousness can lead to smoking habits, drug experimentation and other illegal behaviors. They can also lead to a GED and the authoring of a book called *MIDMEN*.

Flash forward; you become an adult and are capable of selecting your own pursuits. You think to yourself (either consciously or unconsciously), "Fuck those douche bags. I'll show them." And you go after your dreams all hell bent for leather. No shortage of men have become huge successes out of spite. If we haven't come to terms with our need to succeed beyond, and perhaps in spite of, others' expectations by the time we age into MIDMEN, our feelings of inadequacy can intensify the problem.

Winston Churchill had a terrible relationship with his demanding father. Not helping matters was Winston's defined lisp and perceived ADHD. He had trouble in school, albeit the finest school, and his father was quick to label him a disappointment—even going as far as to forbid him from visiting home. His low self-esteem caused him to present the façade of the heavily inflated ego for which he was known all the way into his old age. Winston spent much of his life striving to succeed largely to disprove his father's low opinion of him. He became one of the most powerful and historically important men on Earth as a result.

Experiences like these are certainly not limited to abuses suffered during our youth. In our pre-MIDMAN period we frequently found that our best laid plans never finished getting laid! The average age of divorce for men is 39. This would generally be prior to midlife crises, but could also easily trigger it. If the divorce is initiated by the man's partner he will generally feel a sense of rejection (ya' think?). He will logically feel like he has a little something to defend—his entire sense of self-worth, for instance. His competitive nature could kick into high gear. He could find himself travelling, starting a bold new enterprise, or hooking up with the proverbial sweet young thing. All of these, while providing some small amount of personal satisfaction unto themselves, also tell the world in a beer-drunk boom of a voice, "Oh yeah, who's the loser now?!"

The problem that occurs when our motivation to accomplish things is driven largely by our need to prove ourselves to others rather than ourselves is that we may miss out on the good feelings of success no matter how successful we are. As MIDMEN this unsatisfied feeling is compounded by the realization that the time we still have to please ourselves is diminishing quickly.

To change this, we have to do two things:

1. **Identify all the things we believe we do for others that we are actually doing for ourselves.** For instance, assuming you have expanded your family by choice, remember why you made that choice. Imagine a world without them. If you're employed think about the problems related to not being employed. In most cases you will find that as annoying, enraging, or nonreciprocal as these relationships could potentially be, they are the life you chose for a reason. The things we do in the course of pursuing a life are not selfless. Remember Selfish Selflessness? We often practice it unconsciously. Unless we have been Shanghaied and forced to serve as a MIDMANWHORE in an Indochinese opium den/brothel in Vientiane, Laos as I described in Brian's story *, we are likely to be the person most responsible for our place in society and life. We got what we asked for. Frankly, even Brian is responsible for his own Shanghai-ing. Gallivanting drunkenly around the New Orleans docks during Mardi Gras in a miracle bra, diving fins and a Jason mask? What did he expect?** With rare exception we are responsible for everything that occurs in our lives. We made the choices that have led us down the path on which we now stand. Anything on your "I never shoulda" or your "I shoulda" lists stand as proof of this fact.

   But regardless of how many of the ingredients of our shit sandwich were placed there by our own hand or the fates, we have to figure out the most rewarding way to eat it.

   Pride and well-being are byproducts of your own good work. It's hard to accept that you have done good work without

* *Did the fucking editor cut Brian's story!?*

** Seriously, you missed a good story.

feeling productive, and hard to feel productive when you have not been true to yourself.

2. **Serve yourself.** We are alive every moment we are alive (you can quote me) so there is no real postponement. If we are wise we experience every moment. This doesn't mean you have to achieve some elevated level of Zen, it just means we can't sleepwalk through life and hope to enjoy a feeling of productivity. We are what we are doing, not what we did or are planning to do, so to be productive is simply to simultaneously "do" and "be." John Lennon said, "Life is what happens to you while you're busy making other plans." He didn't say, "I'll live in the moment... in a moment" or "Been here now, done that." We have to produce to feel alive. Producing is a word subject to many definitions, but to feel productive we must affect ourselves. Productivity = personal satisfaction and growth. Personal satisfaction and growth = success.

    Just like feeling productive, feeling successful is reliant on how well we are servicing our own needs and inner goals. By inner goals I mean success in terms of achieving true happiness, not buying an unnecessarily extravagant new car to generate jealousy from friends and strangers. Let me make this crystal clear: SUCCESS DOES NOT RELATE DIRECTLY TO MATERIAL POSSESSIONS! You could be the richest man in the world and still be unsuccessful. Success = $ is bullshit; success = :). (BTW, that's an equal sign, a smiley face and a period, not a drooling emoticon with a Mohawk.) It is the achievement of something that gives us a genuinely good feeling. Of course this genuinely good feeling could be provided by something work-related, and sure, there could be money involved, but the money is more symbol than actual reward. It's easy to confuse the two.

Success does not announce itself. We do not complete an act and suddenly have a hundred Chuck E. Cheese Skee-Ball coupons print out of our asses to trade in for cheap, plastic rewards. Nor can we attain success simply because someone tells us we have been successful; we must acknowledge and confirm our own successes. This means we will only know success when we have personally determined it ourselves. Leonardo da Vinci said that "Art is never *finished*; merely *abandoned*," which would lead one to believe that the artist favored process over result as a barometer for success. To declare ourselves successful we must do yet another two things:

A. **Permit ourselves to be successful.** Modern civilization has engendered within the human race so much discontent that the declaration of one's personal satisfaction actually seems kind of vulgar. When asked how we're doing, we politely answer, "I'm doing great," but nobody assumes it's true. They accept it as a shortcut for "I don't want to talk about it." In New York they answer, "What are you, writing a fucking book?" which also means they don't want to talk about it. If we dare to state "I'm doing great," like we really mean it and follow up with a litany of good news, many people would take it as obnoxious bragging. I like to eavesdrop . . . but I also like to be eavesdropped on, so I think that makes me even. The vast majority of what I pick up when shoving my ear where it doesn't belong is either complaints, vindictive gossip, or the details of someone's physical problems—usually the graphic description of an illness. Side note to fellow restaurant diners; "They found blood in his stool" should never be spoken out loud in public... or, frankly, in private.

   In his bestselling book, *The Power of Now*, spiritual teacher Eckhart Tolle discusses a condition he refers to as the "Pain Body." In short, this means many of us have become reliant on our own pain and discontentment to form the foundation of our lives. But Bruce Springsteen counters in a single line from the too-good-to-be-just-one-song *Badlands*, "It ain't no sin to be glad you're alive." If you are an empathetic person it can be hard to truly enjoy your successes in a world where so many suffer. If this is the case you have to deal with your feelings, which might mean acting charitably to the extent required for your peace of mind. There is no success without our self-permission for success, so we must remove the barriers to it.

As with *every*thing, honesty with ourselves and those around us is mandatory. Feelings of guilt will trump our feelings of success regardless of how small the win we are attempting to acknowledge might be.

B. Succeed! Of course our first reaction to that suggestion is that success is rarely easy and often impossible. That may be true of the success identified by mothers saying things like, "But my other son, the doctor, *he*'s a big success..." But it isn't true in the larger sense. In fact, it may not even be true of "their other son the doctor." This doctor guy might not actually even be a big success. He may be a wonderful doctor but an unhappy person, which immediately removes him from the success category.

Success in its purest form requires no specific action; it requires neither football field nor ball to spike. Success happens on a moment-by-moment basis. Every moment in which we find happiness and personal satisfaction is successful, and every moment that our minds are ruled by fear or discontentment are unsuccessful; it's no more complicated than that. But arranging and perceiving our lives in a way that allows for that feeling of true satisfaction can be a challenge. Organizing our lives, whether it means demanding "me" time to indulge in an activity we enjoy or controlling our radius so that those around us are not combative or disruptive, requires effort. But even here we can find some personal joy in the effort to make the undertaking itself a success.

Consider this; you are headed out to a day of travel. You will need to get to the airport, get through the terminal, wait for the plane to board, board, fly, and get to your hotel. Normally we think about it in terms of certain aspects of the trip being more or less pleasurable than others: the airport shuttle is a drag, finally hitting the hotel room is good, etc. But that is simply untrue. There are no rules that prohibit us from enjoying pretty much every aspect of the trip that doesn't cause us physical pain.

Once in Vietnam my wife and I boarded exactly the kind of bus you imagine boarding in rural Vietnam. We were the only westerners on board and the bus was totally packed. There was a woman lying down in the aisle to sleep with her head right next to my foot. There were people buried under sacks of grain and rice, invisible in their seats, and a driver's assistant whose acrid body was the land that soap forgot. As we settled into our front row seats behind the chain-smoking, dangerously aggressive driver for the four-or-so-hour ride, we popped in our interconnected iPod headphones. Just as our attitudes were about to sour I cranked up the awesomely inappropriate "Vacation" by The Go-Gos. Our raucous laughter confused a lot of people. We actually ended up thoroughly enjoying the ride! *That* is success. Not arriving at the bus's destination; truly enjoying the trip.

We don't succeed on graduation day, or at the completion of any task, we succeed every time we experience a moment of honesty. We even succeed when we cry or mourn if that's the honest reaction to a moment. Success is easy; collecting

> the commonly held trappings of success is hard – and largely unnecessary.

The perception of success is not necessarily evidence of the real thing. I know I dealt with this a little back in THE MONEY when I described the guy with the Aston Martin, but confusion about the reality of success is really huge so I'm going to hit it again in the context of *personal feelings* of success.

One of my closest friends had an experience that really pulled the whole concept of business success versus personal success into perspective for me. My friend, I'll call him Sandy, is a showbiz type. He's been an agent with a top talent agency; a manager; he has produced, written, traveled, lunched and dinnered in Hollywood for a few decades. He's also a thrill-seeker, world traveler and, most importantly, a very honest and decent man. He's financially well-off but not possessing of the kind of unfathomable wealth that often finds its way into the pockets of people in his circles. One morning his phone rings. It's a client/famous travel expert/dear friend of his. It turns out the caller, I'll call him Ringo (Okay, I suck at making up fake names to protect the innocent. Sue me.), had put together a whirlwind, five star luxury tour of deepest darkest Africa for some VERY high powered Hollywood executives and one of them copped out. Sandy was invited to come along for free. The tour was to last eleven days, cost about $28,000 per guest, and leave in about ten hours. Sandy, having enjoyed a considerably less complicated trip to Africa not long before, was well positioned to take the vacant seat on the private jet; he had his shots, etc. So Sandy cleared his calendar and jumped at the offer. It should be noted that Sandy is a MIDMAN who needs little of the direction offered by this book; he is, as I said, upright, has an understanding of the things that matter to him, and actually pursues them.

When Sandy got to the airport he found himself boarding a private luxury jet with a couple dozen serious captains of industry. He thought he'd died and gone to Davos. In attendance were the host who, if you know anything about Hollywood studio big shots you've totally heard of, the CEO of one of the biggest talent agencies on Earth, and a couple dozen other wigs of varying degrees of big. They boarded, were no doubt served some variety of champagne that I will never taste, and lifted off.

Because this was no ordinary trip, the travel was crazy. Chartered flights would bring the *cashpack* to the remotest landing strips (read: unobstructed fields) in the Dark Continent where they would be met by Range Rovers that had pounded over rough terrain for days to meet the flight precisely on time. At every location, luxury tents were set up and executive chefs prepared gourmet meals. Rarely visited tribes staged performances of native dances and bizarre rituals involving bloody mutual flagellations. It was as privileged an access as anyone could ever imagine to a world only seen only by those with preternatural levels of endurance or vast amounts of wealth. Thanks to their host's infinite supply of disposable moolah and generosity, these executives were sliding into the bush as easily as dropping into the conveyor belt Doom Buggies at Disney's Haunted Mansion.

As the Continent revealed its secrets across the 11-days, Sandy noticed something odd; the most powerful of the executives weren't there! Oh, they were physically present. They took the flights, ate the meals, attended the sightseeing opportunities and drank the wines, but they weren't "there." No matter how wondrous the terrain or alien the ritual that filled their proximity, they remained in Hollywood. They never stopped talking about business. Rhino over there? Budget for a slate of films over here. Thatch village of painted warriors? Whatever; we're buying a TV network. They never stopped.

Now it could be argued that these guys totally understood what mattered to them most and brought them joy and weren't letting a trip to Africa get in the way of it. Understood, but it does beg the question, what are we working for? It's ultimately important to have a clear understanding of what it is we're after. One reason for the importance of this is that we could be wrong. If we think we're working for the Aston Martin, or to host a $300,000+ trip to Africa for our buddies, but in fact are perfectly content wrestling over deals in our palatial beach houses, then maybe we can acknowledge that, spare ourselves the malaria medicated nightmares and just build a school in Africa with the $300K.

As I said back in THE REASON, "*It takes a long time to reach a worthy goal but only seconds to utter the words, 'I'm done.' This means you fucking well better enjoy the process of reaching that goal because that is how you spent your life.*" Those executives might have been working that very behavior. They don't give a shit about literally finishing the deal; they're on to the next deal. And clearly they don't give a crap about watching the Mursi tribe whack the shit out of themselves and each other with sticks.

Or, the opposite might be true. They may not be happy at all. They may actually have deep-seated desires that they can't for whatever reason approach, or troubled personal relationships they're actually afraid to confront. Achieving the wrong goals can offer us some interesting rewards but true happiness may not be one of them. At a time in our lives when we're weighing our waning years we may start feeling a little time crunch. We need to achieve some genuine happy.

Reaching a goal is often misunderstood to mean "finishing." Finishing as a concept doesn't work unless you're dead, because you're going to keep on doing *something* until you are, even if it's just the act of dying.

Logothetis Gravatas, the man this book is dedicated to, is 89 years old. He's retired and battling the usual selection of maladies an old Detroit Greek might battle. He's not busy, per se, but he's not finished either. He has his own care to manage, a handful of students to which he teaches precious stone faceting, a social life, and the daily pleasure of deciding on his meals. He is loved and he loves. As long as his mind is active, there is no magical plateau he will ascend to where he just doesn't do anything. Doing nothing doesn't mean you're finished, it means you're depressed. There is no light at the end of the tunnel that blinks the word "done." Unless the Dalai Lama is reading this book, I think it's safe to say that neither one of us is on the fast track to nirvana, which would be the only true, single tunnel-ending light I can think of. Otherwise we will do and do and do, and the last thing we will do is die. BTW, if His Holiness the Dalai Lama is reading this book, I would like to respectfully say, what's up Dalai Lama?

When I was about thirteen and living in Farmingdale, Long Island, we had a patch of woods near the house and in those woods was an entrance to the sewer pipes. The kids in the area would climb into the pipes, which were large enough to crawl through, and spelunk under the whole city. I honestly don't recall any excrement down there, so I guess they were just for water drainage. We could travel literally for miles. Kids would set goals for travel further inside; my sister was particularly intrepid. Distance and direction were measured by counting the small manholes. The manholes were illuminated by the light filtering through the holes in the manhole cover, which, by the way, is also known as a "biscuit." Looking down the narrow tunnel of sewer pipe, we saw what appeared to be a single, glowing light. One would take this to be quite literally the *light at the end of the tunnel.* But what it illustrated was much more important than that; each manhole cover along the miles of sewer pipes illuminated the manhole below it. When looking through the darkness, the light appeared to be solitary—*the* light at the end of the tunnel—but it was in fact a series of lights. That's what goal pursuit is; there is no single light at the end of the tunnel, there is a series of lights. The trick is choosing the tunnels that connect goals that truly satisfy us and avoiding the tunnels that carry excrement.

When crawling through the tunnel of life, there is one very important consideration we need to make: we crawl alone. In life, loved ones and friends and co-workers and, in the event of emergencies, first responders will watch our ass for us, but our *priorities* are ultimately ours alone. The exchange of help and/or support is what makes the world go 'round (actually, according to Isaac Newton, the original motion of the matter which formed the world was spinning and since there is no force to stop it, it's still what makes the world go 'round, but you get my point). When we're driving toward a goal, well-chosen or not, everything in our path can appear to have been put there purely for our exploitation. But the human elements on that path likely have goals of their own. This means we have to be careful. Will our friends help us? Sure. Will they keep on helping us if they feel taken advantage of? Some, maybe, but that's not the MIDMAN way of getting things done.

The inability to discern where your interests end and others' interests begin is called *blurred boundaries*. We have boundaries in our lives. If an alcoholic friend calls in the middle of the night to shoot the shit even though you, like the rest of the world with the exception of the alcoholic friend, have to get up in the morning, that alcoholic is not observing a boundary. He's probably not observing the speed limit either. He's only thinking about his desire to shoot the shit and not your right to sleep. On the flip side, if our personal habits, i.e. being late for things, talking without listening, smelling unpleasant, etc. have cost us friendships, and our inability to observe ourselves objectively causes us to blame our friends for the abandonment, we have a form of blurred boundaries.

There are some circumstances where the practice of blurred boundaries is exempt, like the waiter/customer relationship. The server's concern is your interests, and you are not really supposed to consider theirs beyond your obligation to tip and make lame ass jokes if the server is a cute waitress. But successfully controlling our radius is weighted heavily on our ability to understand the impact we have on others by observing their boundaries, or more simply put, pretending to give a shit. It really doesn't matter if the consideration you display is authentic or bullshit, it will generally serve you better. Selfless Selfishness redux. Engaging and ingratiating yourself has much less to do with acting selflessly and much more to do with inspiring others to act on your behalf as well. But if you can't perceive the needs of others you can't attempt to appeal to them, which prevents you from getting them on your side. That inability to perceive the needs of others due to fixation on your own desires is a symptom of blurred boundaries.

I fervently believe that nothing comes close to motivating a MIDMAN like greedy self-interest. We are all ruled by our inner George Costanza. We MIDMEN were immediately preceded by what Tom Brokaw calls "the Greatest Generation." These people were often associated with their selfless willingness to go to work, go to war and then come home and make this country great. We appreciate and revere them but we are not they. Yes, many heroes walk among us, but your garden-variety 21st century MIDMAN is short on you, you, you and long on me, me, me. This isn't a value judgment; it just is what it is. I don't even think we're completely responsible. Curly Howard, whose monk-like pate grants him full philosopher's credentials, spoke it thusly in the unforgivably Oscar-shunned short film, *Disorder in the*

Court; "I'm a victim of *soikumstance*!" He drove home his point with a spirited volley of nyucks. Nyuck, indeed.

So, where do you end and others begin? To respond to this question we must first accept that the film *The Human Centipede* does not provide a valid answer. Every other sentient being on the planet has priorities that are not yours. Sometimes you can buy someone's priorities (see "*lap dance*" – it's not in this book, I'm just saying see it) but even then it's bullshit because your priorities are still not theirs; your money being introduced to their landlord is their priority. When we blur boundaries we essentially trespass into other people's radiuses. Therefore, it could be argued that the best way to avoid behaving from a position of blurred boundaries is to maintain an ongoing acknowledgment of the radiuses of those surrounding you. When we make consideration of others a habit, our lives improve immeasurably. One of the first steps in forming that habit is accepting that not only do people have their own priorities, most of the time they're nothing like yours. Everyone on Earth is having a completely unique existence, and the assumption that they are reacting in the same way we are to anything is ludicrous. When we assume that someone else feels as we do, we are doing something professional callers of such things call *projecting*.

Psychological projection occurs when someone *projects* their thoughts, desires, emotions, whatever onto someone else's thoughts, desires, emotions, whatever. The term "psychological projection" was something Sigmund Freud came up with so it's also known as "Freudian projection," which I mistakenly thought meant to jut one's beard and pipe forward aggressively. Actually, I once went to a movie theater with a Freudian projector. I felt that the beams of light were actually fucking the projection booth window. Projecting is actually pretty natural in a lot of ways. If we have a certain reaction to something why wouldn't we think others have the same reaction? But everything is subject to subjectivity. I happen to like the smell of horseshit. Would I be wise to assume everyone does? No.

Projection is a leading cause of jealousy and suspicion in our marriages. If we step out on our spouse, or even just really want to, and are prone to projection, it means we can never again trust her because if *we* did it, surely *she'd* do it. This seems like a perfect concept to illustrate with a little story. This one is about a rock and roll couple that met in the 80s.

THE TRAGIC STORY OF OZZIE AND EVA. Ozzie used to manage a rock club. It was the shit, and so was he. Thanks to his astute social networking (analogue style; he networked with people in the flesh) there were lines of people around the block and lines of blow across the bar. Big-haired, blue-eyed, gaunt and adorned with cool dangly shit, he looked like a male version of Brett Michaels. Ozzie didn't just know people; he *was* people. People dropped *his* name. The year was 1987; Ozzie was 25.

Like all guys with big hair who managed rock clubs in 1987, Ozzie met waitresses and rock and roll chicks. His apartment endured the kind of traffic that would have had a small town petitioning for a stoplight. Ozzie had developed a kind of routine, a nightly series of cool-enhancement procedures that would bolster his already enviable reputation and tee up his choice of rock and roll queen for the private after-party. First, he arrived at 10-ish when the line on the street was the longest and walked its length, working it like a political candidate. He surreptitiously palmed off line passes and drink coupons as he collected band demos on cassette. He recognized insiders by their participation in a "psych," his own almost-handshake greeting. Everyone treated him so much like the BMOC (Big Man on Coke) how could he not accept the love? It was here, while working these lines in the frosty half-light of the street that he scoped out his prey. Predisposed as he was to his position, he didn't show his hand when he happened upon a contender. He simply dropped that the club was seeking a new waitress if she happened to know anyone who might be interested, etc. He did this repeatedly along the line and assumed correctly that a fair percentage of the clubby-cute young women he spoke to were interested in the job. He could fall madly in lust but still never offer so much as a line pass because, as the night rolled out, *she* would find *him*. This technique may never actually have failed him.

And so it went, night after night, waitress wannabe after waitress wannabe, Ozzie cranked the Cinderella albums, counted out the registers, and lived the vida coca. But it all changed the night Eva stood on the line. Twenty-one, tall and leggy, skin glistening with the dew of amped-up femininity, Eva wasn't easily ignored. Ozzie's first sight of her whacked him like an Elaine Benes shove to the chest. He was rocked to his cowboy boot heels, the momentum sending him flying into a sizable, unnecessarily grouchy passerby who apparently mistook him for someone named Fuckwad. Eva's first impression of him was as a clumsy oaf apologizing like Jerry Lewis. She would never have been into him had she seen his royal hipness, but this awkward and silly entrance hit her button.

Recovering whatever smooth he could muster, Ozzie attempted the usual rap, but Eva wasn't having it. She called him on his use of position and even saw through the waitress search scam. Ozzie was smitten. He still didn't let her cut the line; in fact, they didn't even go inside, they went straight to a diner. Then they went to Ozzie's. Then they went to breakfast. Then lunch, dinner and the club. Ozzie's daily procedures changed to include her, and together they were the perfect big hair rock and roll couple with the end of the 80s and first half of the 90s as their playground.

Though Ozzie remained convinced that it was his THE MAN status that kept Eva at his side, it could not have been further from the truth.

In fact she was really in love with his most vulnerable qualities and prized every moment he revealed them.

As the 90s flew by their family grew, and before either of them noticed they had regular jobs and three kids. It wasn't a bad life by any definition. Eva took to homemaking even going so far as joining the PTA. Ozzie, now back to calling himself Michael, had gotten himself a job working for a national restaurant/nightclub company. I can't give you the name but it has something to do with being pleased to the point of religious fervor that the workweek has finally ended. He really was a good manager so the company made good use of him. They sent him out to observe and troubleshoot locations throughout the country. As Michael enjoyed daily lunches and dinners at company restaurants he found that his BMOC status was returning in interesting ways. The first way was literal; he was eating a lot and becoming a *big* man! The second was unexpected. His status as main office troubleshooter guy actually made him attractive to the local waitresses. The "C" for coke part wasn't in the picture anymore, but an arguably worse vice was finding its way up the nose of his life: C for "copulate." The long weeks on the road and the weakening of his ego behind age, thinning hair and rising weight left him vulnerable to the welcome advances of the local waitresses, and he succumbed.

Back at home, PTA mom Eva kept her rock dude's girlfriend's body and 'tude, which got her hit on regularly. In spite of her summoning the words MILF or cougar in the minds of every healthy young straight dude who observed her, and the words "hubba hubba!" in the old ones, Eva only had eyes for Michael. She loved him even with the extra padding, but she was getting a sense that he wasn't feeling the same about her. At home he favored popping in a video and hitting the old bongy-boo after the kids went beddy-bye. Eva tried to seduce or encourage him using a woman's preternaturally perfect proportion of pressureless playfulness, but to no avail. Her alliterative advances alienated anew. This left Eva with no choice but to hang out with her friends if she wanted any outside life at all. And that was the beginning of the end.

Michael, saddled with the guilt of his dalliances, observed Eva through a distorted lens. With his slovenly body and cheater's guilt he could only assume that Eva was getting some play on the side. He found it hard to see himself as worthy of a woman like Eva, which led to him to *project* (aha!) that she must feel the same way. Though she had never offered any evidence to suggest it, he was certain that her late nights out with the girls were not girl-exclusive. His mood began to change from simply sullen to passive aggressive and then to combative. He wouldn't question her honor directly or state his fears, instead choosing to simply nitpick about things and start the kinds of arguments that don't give way to make-up sex. While he was away on business chasing tail he'd fume over the fantasy life he had created for her. Even during family time at home he imagined her rapturous in the arms of a faceless stranger as he sat with her cuddling and playing with their children. With absolutely no justification for any kind for suspicion beyond the *projection* of his own bad behavior, he tried and convicted her in the court of his own insecure mind. Their arguments escalated to screaming matches, then physical skirmishes, and finally, divorce.

Eva had never done anything remotely wrong. Her nights out with the girls may have been replete with a little complaining about what she wasn't getting at home (sex was third on the list behind love and laughter), but beyond enjoying the attention, none of the flirtations she received were so much as playfully considered. Michael's adversary in the waning days of his marriage was no one but himself. One day the cloud would lift and he would see this clearly for the first time, but would he take the necessary steps to regain his self-esteem so that he could once again enter into a healthy relationship? Tune in next time on *Days of our Wives*.

Having clear judgment of others requires the ability to accept that their thoughts process, priorities, tastes, etc. are different from ours. I'll say this again; I really like the smell of horseshit.

Nietzsche said, "The snake which cannot cast its skin has to die. As well the minds which are prevented from changing their opinions; they cease to be mind." George Harrison said, "It's all the mind." What we think is, essentially, who we are. So if we want to be different than we are, we have to start by thinking differently. The idea that the mind is not malleable is rubbish. To utter a statement like, "Well, that's just how I am" is embarrassingly ignorant and fools no one. We can all change and we all know it so when one of us professes not to have that ability everyone smells the horseshit, whether they enjoy it or not.

Chapter 10

THE BODY

"I finally have the body I want. It's easy, actually, you just have to want a really shitty body."

Louis C.K.

THE BODY

Don't look down; some evil shit is happening to your body. Actually, you can look all you want but you won't be able to see it all. The hair and the gut you can see are just symptoms. The truly evil shit is happening to your body at a cellular level. Even if you're a health nut you can't thwart the onward march of your DNA's predispositions, or what I like to call life's practical joke. As young immortals, we had no reason to waste valuable time considering the schedule of decomposition our genes planned for us, but now as MIDMEN, we're probably taking pause. Mother Nature and Father Time's ageless son Peter Pun (yeah, bitches; I just used the word pun *as* the pun! Shitty joke geeks, I am now your master) has played a terrible trick on us. Our minds, tastes and styles have all remained pretty much intact, but everything south of the cranium is Karachi.

From our skin through our muscle mass and all the way into our light and fluffy nougat centers, every cell is changing. Sometimes our cells change for the better, but generally our cells change for the worse. If our "cells" are only changing because we've been transferred to another prison, aging is the least of our worries. Gerontologists are the scientists who study aging at the cellular level, and they are thrilled with the advances in science that have made so much more information available. Clearly they haven't considered that all that new bad news will eventually apply to them.

The National Institutes of Health shares some dispiriting findings on their website. They explain that our cells age at different rates, but add that no one here gets out alive (yes, in this example Jim Morrison worked for the National Institutes of Health). Some of the real early causes of aging include:

- Loss of lung tissue elasticity and shrinkage to the muscles of the rib cage, which decrease your air intake.
- Reduction in the production of digestive enzymes in the stomach, making it tougher to digest nutrients, the digestion of which is rumored to be a good thing.
- The blood vessels in the heart get hard (hey, at least *something* still does) and collect fatty deposits.
- I'm guessing you already noticed the decreased sperm production?
- The prostate starts growing into a bocce ball.
- Instead of "splitting" as in reproducing, cells start "*splitting*" as in departing like a beatnik with better things to do.
- Numbers of immunity cells decline, creating a lovely opportunity for evil cells, like cancer, to make themselves at home.
- Bone and joint density decreases, as opposed to when we were young and we would *smoke* a joint then bone *someone*.

The list seriously goes on forever. Most of this stuff isn't new information for you; chances are that as you've been aging you have also been inadvertently preparing for a degree in biology. With each physical problem we suffer personally and every emergency our friends and family have, we learn more and more about anatomy and medicine. To prove my point I present . . . another fucking quiz! Actually, this is the first real quiz in the book since it contains right and wrong answers. Relax, it's multiple choice.

THE *ARE YOU A DOCTOR AND DIDN'T EVEN KNOW IT?* QUIZ

Below you will find a series of common maladies or cures. Read the clue and select which choice applies to it. There is no time limit, but you're not getting any younger...

	A	B	C	D
A bulging disc between L3 and L4 can cause:	Sciatica	Unconsciousness	Tennis elbow	Compliments
A CPAP machine is recommended for:	Heart Monitoring	Magnetic Imaging	Sleep Apnea	Personal Hygiene
A benign tumor is one that is:	Over one centimeter	Harmless	On skin	Between B-8 and B-10
A colonoscopy:	Looks at the colon	Listens to the colon	Measures the colon	Is the name of Colin Powell's biography
The appendix:	Creates adrenalin	Aids digestion	Balance metabolism	Is a worthless evolutionary relic

The answers are, A, C, B, A and D. If you weren't able to answer these correctly, you have led a charmed life. But assuming you have answered correctly, you can see that we obtain a great deal of medical knowledge just by living long enough. You can probably also tell when "that's gonna need some stitches," or someone's having a heart attack, or, if you're any kind of citizen, detect a stroke.* Understanding the aging process and the physical ramifications thereof is just part of the knowledge base you need to clear your slate for indulging in what you have determined actually matters to you. If you think getting true value out of your life is tough with mental distractions, try it with physical ones! Pain makes everything harder, so that's a gimme, but diet and lack of exercise could be sapping your energy, and your physical appearance could be undermining your confidence. This chapter is all about how to get our shit together physically so we can party all the way to our own funerals.

Guys "our" age rarely feel as healthy as they did when they were younger because they're simply not. Suffice it to say we literally aren't

* F.A.S.T. is an easy way to remember the sudden signs of stroke. **F**ace drooping – does one side of the face droop or is it numb? **A**rm weakness – is one arm weak or numb? **S**peech difficulty – is speech slurred? **T**ime to call 911!

the men we used to be. However, in most cases not involving illness, our feeling shittily is the product of our own habits and lifestyle. We don't just miss out on feeling good when we practice habits like habitual smoking, problem drinking or compulsive overeating; we cheapen our lives. This is an area where midlife crisis and depression cross over. Both conditions inspire lethargy and unhealthy instant gratification. "Fuck this, I'm going out to have a cigarette," is a common example of a self-destructive reaction to an already less than life affirming situation. This unfortunate imaginary sample dude is gifting himself with a little treat to convince himself he can enjoy a moment. "I dieted all day and now I want to eat some kind of greasy shit!" The very idea of harming our bodies as a form of self-reward requires serious consideration. We know innately what is good for us, yet we stubbornly maintain that we are better off not exercising, or eating crap or whatever behavior is bad for us. Our stomachs grumble and our doctors prescribe medications but we're still all, "Hey, my body ain't telling *me* what works better around here!" Dude, if you can't take orders from your own body, you have a serious problem with authority!

The seven deadly sins are lust, gluttony, greed, sloth, wrath, envy and pride. Really? How about: No, Yes, Yes, Yes, Yes, No, No. Not only aren't envy and pride sins, deadly or otherwise, I think they're actually helpful! Gluttony, greed, sloth and wrath have all shown up at parties I've thrown and they're complete buzzkills, but where would we be without the other three? Okay, lust? Bring it on. Would we ever have done anything after, say, 12 years old if it weren't for lust? Would we have thought about our clothing, our attitude, or our personal aroma if it weren't for our desire to get ourselves within smelling distance of another, frequently softer, human being?

And envy? How would we know what we want unless we saw someone else with it? Envy isn't just about physical possessions. We can envy experience, wisdom, prowess, anything. Sax players who envy Charlie Parker are the greatest sax players who ever lived. Envy is a perfectly acceptable motivator.

How could *pride* be a deadly sin? Let's say you've been a dedicated and attentive father and your youngest son, Beaver, is graduating at the top of his middle school class (that's right, in this example you're Ward Cleaver). How could that feeling be a sin? Actually, the deadly sin editors do generally pair pride with arrogance, which I'll give them.

Vanity gets grandfathered into the deadly sin top seven by being a component of pride, but vanity, if properly harnessed, is the most powerful ally we have to get our shit together physically. Think about this: if we were really concerned with our appearance, the byproduct would be that we remain fit, watch our posture, display rows of well-tended teeth and employ so many other healthy habits. Remember the story of Ozzie and Eva? He was all, like, fat and adulterous and she was all, like, hot and honest and he was all, "No way she's not also all adulterous" and got, like, all jealous and totally broke up his marriage. Ozzie broke two cardinal rules: one, he fucked around and two, he let himself go. If he had kept his dick in his pants and his body in shape he would still have the best deal he was going to get.

I have tried to keep this book from being too autobiographical, notwithstanding a few brief anecdotes (coughing into hand three times, "*gym-shower-boner*"), but here I think my personal experience could be of help. I am vain. Terribly, terribly vain. Back in the 80s and into the early 90s I made my living as an entertainer and kind of a pretty boy at that, so I got in the habit of really giving a shit about how I looked. Now that I think about it, I was probably less vain and more plain ol' girl crazy. Regardless of my M.O., health wasn't my objective—looking good was, but the habits required ultimately directed me toward a much healthier lifestyle. As with burning calories, age has made my quest to look good increasingly challenging and, in some ways, fruitless, but my stubborn self-awareness continues to win me raves from my doctor after every annual physical. My blood pressure is perfect, all of my readings are right in the groove, and my 55-year-old prostate is boyishly petite and as smooth as a hardboiled egg.

In the following sections we're going to look at some broader information about exercise, grooming and diet. Pick and choose as you will, but there is scientific evidence to guide you. People's flexible acceptance when it comes to science is puzzling. If we required surgery, we would of course prefer to have it performed by the world's leading specialist, but when the world's leading specialists tell us that fast food is poison, or that lack of exercise causes as many deaths as smoking, or that *smoking* causes as many deaths as smoking, they're pretentious fools—or worse, un-American (which is a fair point since many experts are not American). If that's where our mindset is, we need to get over it or accept that we willfully act on self-destructive decisions made with faulty data. The choice is ours.

Of course not all of the following will apply to everyone in the same way. I'm sure some alert-enough-to-be-scared-shitless readers have already cleaned up their act. Also, this is just an overview. There may not be too many versions of "Modern Men's Guides to Surviving Midlife Crisis" out there, but there's a ton of material on exactly this subject so you won't have to dig too deep pursuing more information.

It feels like it's been too many pages since we considered this:

1. I'm actually getting old.
2. It's ultimately going to suck.
3. Tough shit. I will still need to live life to the fullest until I can't anymore.

While the random nature of things is always a factor, we do have the power to exert some control over the conditions set forth in item 3 of the little mini-contract above. We can make our lives fuller, but like any tough job it takes a tender chicken, no, scratch that; it takes a tough man. The preceding chapters have explored the challenging conditions around us that might be preventing us from obtaining a little self-gratification (another do-it-yourself masturbation joke!). Honesty was, in every instance, integral to the successful reshaping of those situations in our favor. Acting as a proper custodian of our own physical being demands that we be brutally honest with ourselves. I'm not going to ask you to stand in front of a mirror naked; in fact, I'm going to beg you not to. If you insist on it, I would respectfully request you leave this book in another room. The human body provides the perfect CSI-ready crime scene for the self-observant. It's pretty much all going to be there, the good news and the bad. Especially as pertains to age.

Since I've asked you to remain clothed, we will chart time's assault on our bodies with the help of da Vinci's Vitruvian Man.

Okay, rhetorical question: what is the first sign of aging on a guy? *BZZZZZZ*! Sorry, time's up: hair loss. Conversely, it can make old guys like Vitruvius look much younger. But remove the hair and…

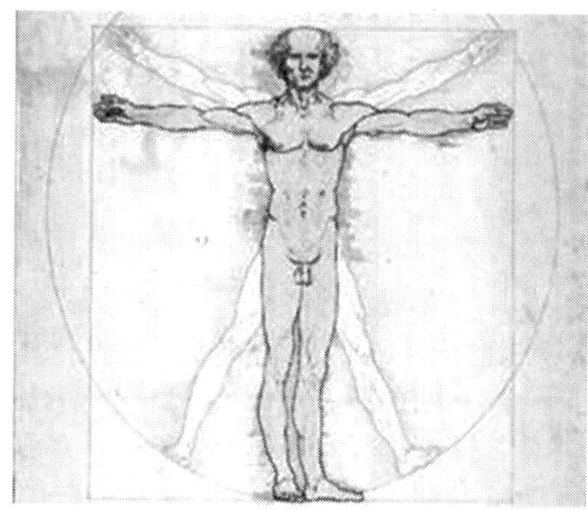

Actually, I don't think we actually *lose* the hair at all! What happens is this: the hair grows back into the head and travels through the skull, then down through the neck into the body where it starts popping out from the ears, nose, eyebrows, shoulders, stomach, back, feet, freakishly high on the cheekbones, then finishes us off with a rainforest of thatch on our taints.

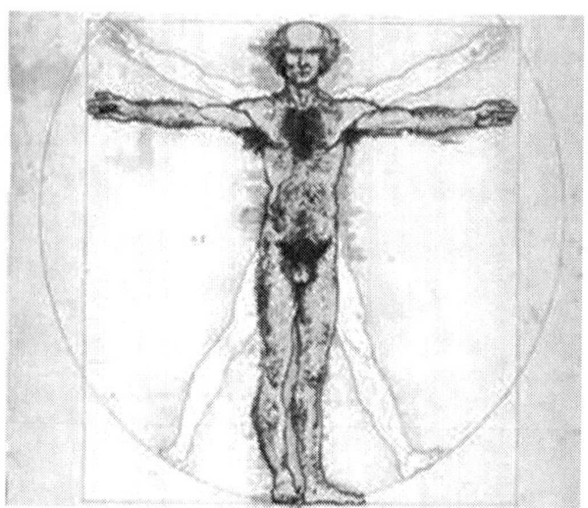

While hair loss and gain locations are fairly obvious, poor eyesight is a little harder to deduce, unless you're watching a MIDMAN try to read small print. Then out come the glasses.

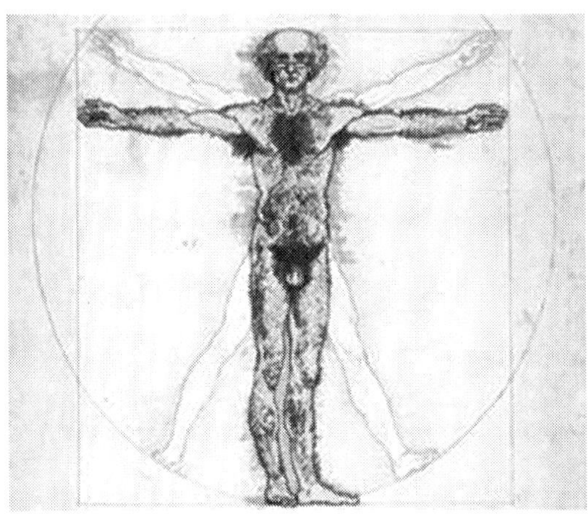

There are three major problems with reading glasses. The first is remembering where they are. I finally said fuck it and put a pair in every room of the house… except, of course, for the one where I happen to be when I need them. The second is vanity. They scream middle-aged louder than pretty much anything else on Earth, except an earring. The third problem is that they turn Vitruvian Man into Bob Newhart. What MIDMEN wants to wear these things when he's out? I won't do it. If I'm at the grocery store and the cashier puts a receipt in front of me, I just sign it. Half the time I'm signing the conveyor belt. The cashier is basically on the honor system because I'm not putting on the glasses. If midlife crisis is like a second puberty, then reading glasses are like pubic hairs; they're popping out more but I'm not ready for anybody to see them.

Of course the good news is if you can't find your glasses, all of your friends have a pair. They're interchangeable. You can go to a restaurant with a group of people your age and just pass one pair around the table and each take turns looking at the menu. It's like the new joint, "Hey, don't Bogart those 1.75s!"

Hopefully Vitruvius didn't need a hearing aid since nothing like that would be available to him for another 500 or so years. Sadly, chances are he did. After 55 the hearing starts seriously going to shit. And that's for anyone, Buddha. The loudest thing Buddha ever heard were his own Bodhi leaf farts. MIDMEN have attended a cumulative 16 *GAZZILLION* rock concerts, so we are screwed. Ironically, while age is making our hearing worse, our ears actually get bigger.

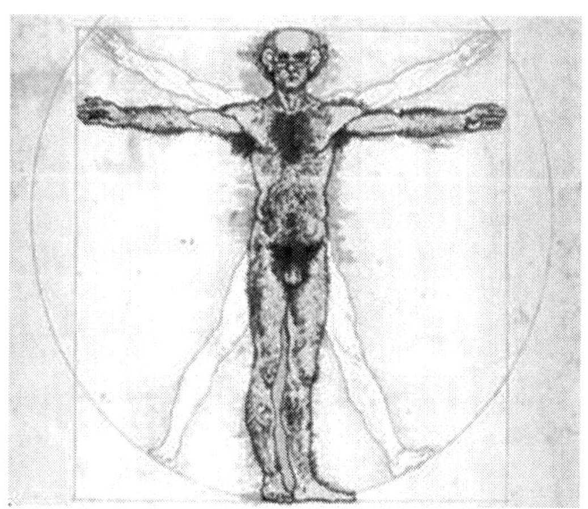

And while this is happening your nose gets bigger and your sense of smell is going. And your teeth spread out, so basically a MIDMEN isn't just in the process of getting old, he's also becoming grotesque.

Your brain is shrinking. At 30 the brain starts losing a lot of its weight. As reported by the National Institutes of Health, "The volume of the brain and/or its weight declines with age at a rate of around 5% per decade after age 40 with the actual rate of decline possibly increasing with age particularly over age 70."

When the brain shrinks, bad shit like chance of stroke and dementia also increase. The Institute suggests that you can help keep your brain pleasingly plump by reducing cardiovascular risk with stuff like "regular exercise, a healthy diet, and low to moderate alcohol intake." They also say you need to keep your brain busy. That couch and its evil accomplice, the TV, are out to kill you. Preparing yourself to indulge in what matters to you will save your life. It's no less than that.

Okay, so all that weight we're losing in our brains? Well, apparently it's following the path forged by our hair and creeping southward. But unlike the hair, this weight is making a beeline right for our asses. Between brain shrinkage and ass growth, by the time you're 45 your ass is bigger and smarter than you are.

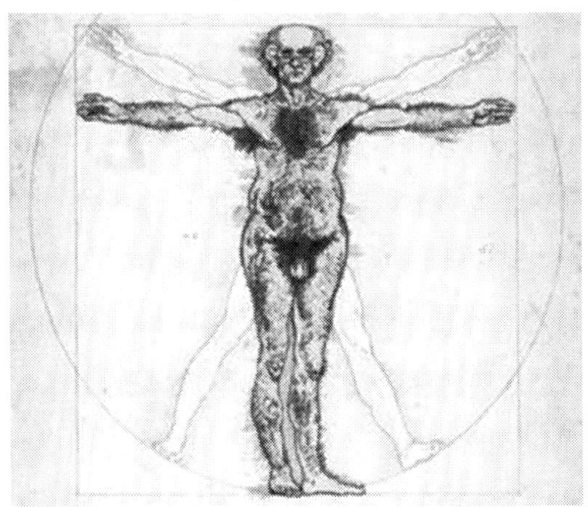

Between the ages of 30 and 70, muscle mass declines more than 20% in men who don't work out regularly. Bone density also diminishes starting round 35. I'll be getting into exercises in the EXERCISE section below, but the loss of muscle and bone density offers too sweet an opportunity to further deface our Vitruvian dude.

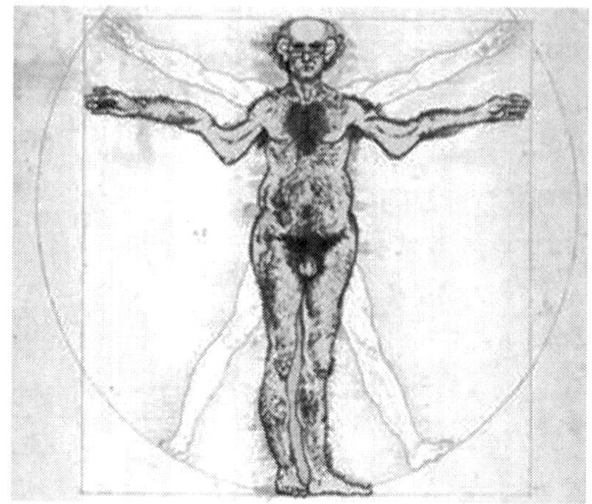

According to Webster's, the word *entropy* describes "a process of degradation or running down or a trend to disorder," making it the perfect word to explain the MIDMAN's body. That extra poundage that may have found its way onto your person, which I earlier explained as being caused by a bad diet, *also* has an evil accomplice. Our muscles burn calories, so when we lose them, the calories hang around. This means that unless we maintain or improve our muscle mass, we are going to start gaining weight.

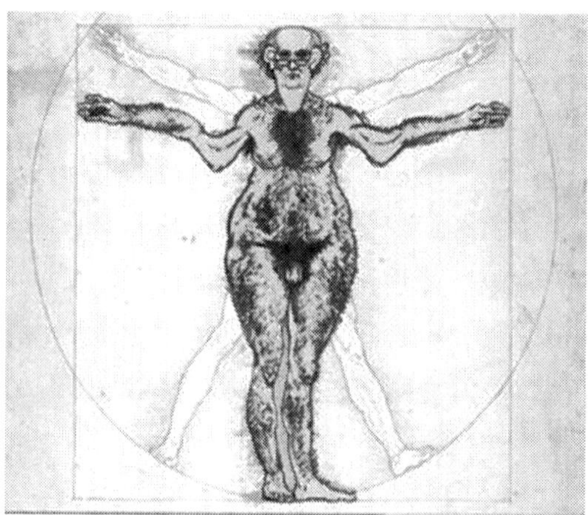

More than one-third of U.S. adults are obese and the rate is highest among middle-aged adults 40-59 years old. MIDMANing can be strenuous business. I don't know your personal "what matters" motivation, but if it requires you to be ambulatory, you may want to take the upcoming DIET and EXERCISE sections below seriously. But even if you do everything right—exercise, diet, meditate, save a village from a disease, carry a puppy out of a burning building, or wear tighty whities 24/7—there's no way to prevent this:

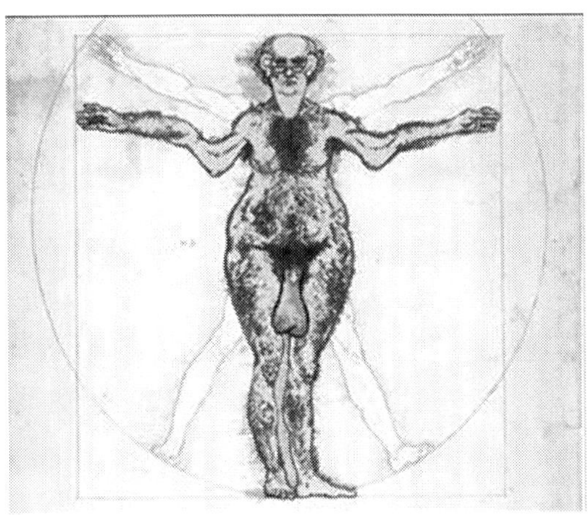

DIET

Adults put on about a pound a year, which means estimating the weight of a guy's spare tire is like counting the rings in a tree trunk. The Harvard School of Public Health conducted a definitive study on this very subject and found that diet plays a far greater role in adult weight gain than even exercise. Apparently we eat more shit as we age. It seems inconceivable to me that we *could* eat more shit than when we were younger!

If, as the statistic above would suggest, we are carrying around a few extra pounds we don't want, the commonly held way to address the problem is to go on a diet. But dieting is bullshit. You don't go *on* a diet, you change your diet. Granted, Sinatra smoked and drank his way to 82-years-old and Jim. Fixx, who authored "The Complete Book of Running," died while, well, running at 52. So why watch your diet?

The key to understanding how to eat is to acknowledge that we are running a machine. If our bodies were cars and called for gasoline we wouldn't fill their tanks with Slurpees. Well our bodies may not be cars, but it turns out we still shouldn't try to run them on Slurpees! We have to think before we fill.

Notwithstanding leisurely meals, eating is a pain in the ass. We have to stop doing what we're doing, procure food, get it in us, and then go back to what we were doing. Grabbing the easiest, quickest, cheapest thing is pretty understandable. But the easiest, quickest, cheapest thing is usually unadulterated fucking garbage. It's a Slurpee cleverly disguised as meat and bread. This means we can't just mindlessly seek out our sustenance like zombies mindlessly gobbling... minds. We have to fuel up correctly.

The benefits of eating properly should appeal to the self-serving part of all of us. A healthy diet prevents all kinds of maladies from high blood pressure to diabetes. My former accountant, may he rest in peace – he's very much alive, just retired – has spent the majority of his life as an avid golfer. His two favorite aspects of golfing were winning and a cheeseburger lunch, both of which he enjoyed pretty much every day . . . until the quintuple bypass! He's back to golfing but the burgers are a much rarer treat; clarification, he doesn't eat them bloody, he eats them *infrequently*.

Virtually all of the food I see as a resident of a western country is bad for me. All the popular fast food is crap. It's all salt, sugar, processed meat and GMO-sullied lettuce and flour. My eyes no longer perceive it as food. If I see a Burger King, I may as well be looking at a dry cleaner for all the dining options it offers me. Anything made with factory farmed meat is likely to come with a bonus hit of antibiotics. I should disclose at this juncture that I'm a pescatarian. Humans require some animal protein so I eat fish and seafood but no other animals. But that doesn't mean I think all meat is poison. There are farms out there feeding their animals well, offering them a decent life and even killing them humanely. That killing part matters. Intelligent animals (pigs are smarter than dogs) are terrified when they're being slaughtered and it makes them release a cocktail of hormones and toxic substances that don't cook out.

One of the great rules I find myself inadvertently following is that we should never shop in the middle of the supermarket. Hit the organic fruit, the bakery (whole grains, always) and then the dairy, maybe the meat, then get the hell out. All that shit in the middle, the sweetened cereals, the prepared, processed rice mixes, Hamburger Helper, or canned any-fucking-thing save organic beans, don't even look at it. Move along, nothing to see here.

The fight gets tough when we try to eliminate the things from our life that we identify as rewards. As I wrote above, we tend to "treat" ourselves to things that are bad for us. "I was good on my diet yesterday so today I'm going to enjoy some greasy, gross animal byproducts." "I worked late so I'm going to unwind in front of the TV with my roommates Ben and Jerry." Eating correctly is less a switch you flip on and off and more an act of self-honesty; a schizophrenic self-intervention. The come to Jesus moment in a MIDMAN's physical preparation to fight for some of what matters is when he faces the cold hard facts about food. Almost all the food making itself easily available to us is working against our well-being.

In hopes of making you an alert-enough-to-be-scared-shitless reader, we'll start with a list of foods you probably didn't know were cancer causing. Bon appétit!

- Microwave popcorn. Actually, not the popcorn itself so much. The "butter" in the bag contains diacetyl, which is known to cause cancer and possibly damage to the lungs. And the *bag* is lined with an EPA certified carcinogen that research has found leads to liver and pancreatic cancer, infertility and tumors. Buy an electric popper.
- Non-organic fruits are saturated with pesticides and fertilizers. It's rampant on apples, but really no non-organic is entirely safe.
- Processed meats are dog food, you know it and you've always known it. Hot dogs? Bacon? (I know, "*Not bacon?!*") Lunch meats aren't even dog food. They're all packed with sodium, which you knew, and carcinogenic chemicals.
- Red meat, even if it's organically grown. According to reporting from *WebMD*, "People who had red meat two to three times as often as white meat had about a 50% higher risk of developing colon cancer." Side note; if you've reached 50 and haven't gotten a colonoscopy, man up and do it. It's not that bad (getting ready for it kind of sucks, but the procedure is nothing).
- Farmed fish. They're basically grown like crops, replete with pesticides and all the other dirty tricks. *Le poisson est un poison.*
- Potato chips and the like. Shit, shit and shit. Trans fats, crazy salt, and here's the mystery guest: acrylamide, a delicious carcinogen also found in cigarettes!
- Sodas of all kinds. Sure, you got your derivative 4-methylimidazole (4-MI) for all your cancer-causing needs, but soda would help you grow cancer even if it didn't try to cause it! It acidifies our bodies, which feeds cancer cells no matter what got them going.

- GMOs. Japan, New Zealand, Germany, Ireland, Austria, Hungary, Greece, Bulgaria, Luxembourg and huge swathes of many other countries have banned this crap. Tests on genetically modified organisms have shown that they cause birth defects and rapid tumor growth in research animals. Good luck finding soybeans, wheat, and corn, that haven't been grown with them.
- Refined sugars. Cancers love 'em more than kids!
- Diet anything. "Diet" usually translates to "aspartame," which causes cancers, birth defects, and heart problems.

So don't eat those! But you still have to eat, so here's a list of healthy stuff commonly known as "superfoods" also courtesy of *WebMD*: Beans, blueberries, broccoli, oats, oranges, pumpkin, salmon (not farmed), soy, spinach, tea (green or black), tomatoes, turkey, walnuts, and yogurt. Establishing good eating habits doesn't mean you have to starve or start looking anemic.

Start by cutting meat out of all but one meal a day and, whenever you can, make that meat wild caught fish or seafood. Beans and legumes in a million varieties, eggs, nuts and all those meaty but not really meat products made with soy and tempeh are great ways to get your protein (and most of them are also great fiber sources, nudge, nudge, wink, wink).

Vegetables you should know about, right? We've all been hearing "eat your vegetables" our whole lives. We just need to do it. While you should do your best to buy organic, even the most poisonous and gene-mutating are chockfull of vitamins, minerals and fiber. Vegetables are great for those little meals as the day goes along because you eat a lot of them and you'd be unlikely to take in more calories than you'd burn, assuming they're not cheese-slathered. You won't need the cheese anyway because dark green leafy vegetables, especially broccoli, bring the calcium.

If you're still eating some meat, you're probably going to get the fats you need. But if, like me, you eschew eating land animals, you have to choose fats that are high in omega-3 fatty acids. Nuts or seeds or nut butter or olive or canola oil would all do the trick.

Like exercise and grooming, we're probably more likely to be motivated by what we see on the outside than what we don't see on the inside. The typical MIDMAN is far more likely to have his day ruined by a zit than by the buildup of plaques in his major arteries. Out of sight, out of mind. Vanity, once again is a virtue. Since I am your vain guide to vain vanity, here's what foods run through my . . . veins.

First and foremost, I don't drink sweetened beverages, diet or otherwise. All sweetened drinks are a bad deal calorie vs. results-wise. A can of Coke has 140 calories and 38 grams of sugar, which is the equivalent of ten sugar cubes. To its credit, Coke has 34 grams of caffeine. If your eye is on the caffeine, a 16 oz. McDonald's coffee (which, if you learned anything in the money chapter, is what you should be drinking instead of paying some barista's tuition) has 100 mg of caffeine and if you drink it black, zero calories. Even juice, unless it's freshly squeezed, is shit. The journal *Lancet Diabetes & Endocrinology*, the gossip rag for diabetes fanboys, published a report noting, "…that because of its high sugar content, fruit juice could be just as bad for us as sugar-sweetened beverages like carbonated drinks and sodas."

The portion-size Nazis say that your piece of meat (or whatever protein) should be the size of a deck of cards. You pair that with all the veggies you want and some kind of starch like a baked potato and you're looking good. This may not fill you entirely if you have been eating big American portions, so use the veggies to bulk things up and lighten up on the meat. Dessert is still possible if you go with fruit or at least 100% fruit sorbet. Also, think before you chomp. An Oreo, one measly Oreo, has 65 calories. NOT worth it! There's a great rule that you should only eat until you're 80% full because in 20 minutes your brain will fully understand what your mouth and stomach have been up to and send out the "full" signals.

One of the functions of eating food is keeping our blood sugar balanced. If we don't eat often enough we can suffer from low blood sugar. That means either you have a small meal every three hours or a temper tantrum every five. These little protein-based snacky mealy deals reboot your metabolism. Dangerously low blood sugar is known as hypoglycemia and it's a pretty common condition. People who suffer from hypoglycemia, of which there are many and of which I am one, face some dangerous symptoms. They can get dizzy then start shaking and sweating—pretty much all the stuff that happens in an Elvis song. The most obvious symptom we can observe in a hypoglycemic or whose someone whose blood sugar has dropped is that he (read, I) will act like a total asshole. Trust me on this; at least half the time you act like a dick it's because your blood sugar is low. Here's a little radius control tip: tell everyone you know that you have a blood sugar problem. I've got people feeding me wherever I go; friends and family. They all have a vested interest in not letting my Dr. Jekyll go all Mr. Hyde.

My wife has a theory that people who get road rage in traffic get it because traffic occurs in the morning when the driver may have missed breakfast, or on the way home in the evening after lunch has worn off. I told her it was a stupid fucking theory and that she should leave that kind of shit to the experts. She made me a sandwich.

If you want to head the problem off at the pass, don't wait until you're hungry. Use the clock, not your stomach. You're better off eating a few small meals throughout your day than the three squares we were taught about all our lives. We'll burn our fuel more efficiently that way and stave off low blood sugar.

Books like this one, magazines and websites can offer all the dietary advice in the world, but if you're not ready to deal with your health realistically, it just doesn't matter. That's why I advocate for vanity; book something social, maybe even a bathing suit-wearing event with people you'd like to impress, and let your ego guide you through the process of getting awesome looking. Better still: picture a world where more people actually want to have sex with you!

EXERCISE

MIDMEN are notorious couch potatoes and couches kill. Guys our age who spend two or more hours a day watching the tube (how old *are* we? TVs don't even *have* tubes anymore) are 125% more at risk of a heart attack than guys who watch less. Four or more hours? Those guys are 48% more likely to die of any cause. And now, thanks to the new "sit your ground" laws, a couch can kill you and totally get away with it.

The benefits of exercise extend into every aspect of our lives. How we choose to exercise is very personal and the wrong choice can put us off it again. We shouldn't assume that the sports we played in school are the perfect physical outlet for us today. Remember, professional athletes retire much younger than you probably are right now. But if you have a sport you love, there's no reason not to use that as incentive to help get you in shape. Just join a local league. Of course some of the younger guys can take these things a little too seriously, so make sure the commitment doesn't invite new bad vibes into your life. My wife played softball on a local league and found herself surrounded by some seriously intense dudes. She should have seen it coming; the name of the team was the Simi Valley Spoil Sports. The bar that sponsored them had a bouncer and an EMT. Their logo was a broken bottle. She couldn't quit until her replacement was paroled.

Baseball, football, and basketball fantasy camps offer a great incentive to shape up and could also tick an item off your bucket list. The guys who go to those are your age, meet some of their idols, and get their asses kicked a little with workouts. Or there's the gym, jogging in the streets, biking, luging (works even better than fiber, wink, wink) and on and on.

Having some idea of what we'd like to look like really helps. We all have our own concept of what our ideal body would be. I remember once seeing a guy at the beach who was completely ripped from the waist up, but like, angry Lou Ferrigno-chested big, and had legs that looked like pool cues. No muscle on them at all. But he was strutting around as if he looked sane, so apparently he had reached his ideal. Yours will be different (but please promise me it won't be the buffed out chest and pool cue look).

Dr. William H. Sheldon was a psychologist and Harvard professor back in the 1930s and 1940s. Though he was primarily interested in figuring out how body types were related to personality characteristics like introversion and extroversion, he ended up developing a body type classification system called somatyping. He designated the three primary types as ectomorphs, endomorphs and mesomorphs. Each of us is one of those. Knowing which can really help guide our diet and our exercise program. I have categorized my diet and exercise suggestions by somatype. Find yourself.

Ectomorphs: Joey Ramone, Jim Carrey, Conan O'Brian

Like a tofu hotdog, ectomorphs are long, thin and totally meat free. These are the guys who can't put on weight no matter how much crap they eat or beer they drink. They have a medical condition many of us know as "fuck you." While the ectomorphs' high metabolism may have its advantages in terms of regulating body mass, it isn't a panacea. These guys can't put on muscle very well.

Gym rats call ectomorphs "hard-gainers" because of their thyroid-dominant system, paired with a sympathetic nervous system that revs like a well-tuned 'Vette. So how does a guy who can't gain weight or put on muscle gain weight or put on muscle? He tweaks his diet and does the exercises that work for his frame.

DIET TWEAKS: If you're working out, it's carbs, carbs and more carbs. But if you're not, it's not. The healthy dietary habits outlined in the DIET section above pertain to all three body types during periods of normal energy use, but the ectomorphs need lots more carbs for weightlifting or running or whatever. They burn it faster so they need to feed the fire.

EXERCISE: Trying to build big muscles on the lithe frame just doesn't work and will end in frustration, with the ectomorph crying and palm punching the wall like an angry little girl. So don't go big; go wiry. The ectomorph's frame is the rock star/cool guy frame, so work it. Lyle Lovett, Sid Vicious, and Keith Richards rock the ectomorph style, while Johnny Depp, Matthew McConaughey and Ryan Reynolds actually pull off action hero roles. So how do ectomorphs get some muscle on those bones? According to *Fitness Magazine*, it's totally possible.

- Only work out three to four days a week if you're weight training, otherwise you're into diminishing returns.
- The body produces increased levels of testosterone and growth hormone for around 45 minutes. Go much longer and you'll start producing cortisol, which breaks down muscle tissue and you don't want that.
- Do 8–12 reps per set (with breaks between sets). I won't get into the science, because it's above my pay grade, but it's good for you.

We'll get into what works for all body types later, but these tips should get ectomorphs on their way to beefing up a bit. Of course consistency is mandatory.

Endomorphs: Russell Crowe, William Shatner, Jason Alexander

The words we're looking for here are "husky" or "stocky," or "unusually hungry." When you hear a heavy person explain their weight by saying they have big bones, they're essentially saying they're endomorphs. That's only if it's plural. If they say they have a *big bone*, singular, politely excuse yourself and back out of the men's room.

Endomorphs tend to be heavier guys. They put on weight and muscle easily. This type of body and metabolism is a blessing and a curse. It's a blessing because endomorphs can have a really great build, but a curse because they pack on the pounds really easily if food isn't being converted into muscle. Linebacking is a good job for endomorphs but generally not easy to just show up and apply for.

DIET TWEAKS: Limit your carbs. Maybe you have an ectomorph locked in the basement that you could feed them to. Pancakes, pasta, potatoes and the like? Not your friends. Non-starch vegetables, however, are your friends so eat what we amateur dietitians call, "a shit load."

Endomorphs need to eat like they're hypoglycemic, so several small meals throughout the day instead of three bigger ones. Diet control-wise, if you can pull off keeping an approximate mental count of your calories, try to stay under 1500/day. If you're actually working out then hit more of the healthy fats like nuts, eggs, cheese and like that. Meat has some bad fats and, unless you're careful, antibiotics and other crap, so limit it (though fish has those great omega-3s and good fat so, you know, yum). As always, avoid farmed fish.

EXERCISE: Endomorphs are the bizarro ectomorphs; everything is the opposite. This means burning calories is a serious issue. Choose your poison: running, walking, biking, or elliptical machines; pretty much anything but golf. That is, unless when you golf you chase the ball in a full-out run, which would be pretty fucking funny to watch.

- Cardio matters. There is nothing on, in or around your body that won't benefit from 45 minutes of something aerobic every day. You need about 20 minutes of aerobic activity just to burn through your glycogen, which is the energy reserve you burn before body fat. So if you can pull off 30-45 minutes of jogging or even fast walking, everything after the first 20 minutes is the good stuff. Even three or four sessions a week would make a big difference.
- Strength Training. Unless they work as bouncers or play for the Simi Valley Spoil Sports, endomorphs don't want to try and get big muscles. They're already big guys and the muscles just exaggerate that. But they still need muscle because that's how we burn fat. Remember what happened to Vitruvius when he had no muscles? Not pretty.

  The trick is to keep weights low and reps high. This way muscle is toned, not enlarged, so calories are burned efficiently but the bulk doesn't get any bulkier.

Mesomorphs: George Clooney, Hugh Jackman, Will Smith

This is kind of the money category. Guys who are mesomorphs are born with the root elements of a good body and good metabolism to boot. They can gain and lose weight easily, build muscle with a minimum amount of effort, and when they go out all the ladies in the house say, "Whoot-whoot!"

Really, beyond all the science and whoot-whooting, this is just a medium build. In sports these are your tennis players, your figure skaters, and even body builders tend to come from this group.

DIET TWEAKS: Unless the mesomorph wants to build muscle, your standard healthy diet will do the trick. But if he does want to gild the lily, all he needs to do is make sure he goes lean. Low fat proteins like eggs, Greek yogurt and seafood make the muscles happen. Add some complex carbs like whole grains, green veggies and fruit, toss in some beans for fiber and everything should be working nicely.

EXERCISE: Again, the mesomorphs don't need pain to gain when it comes to muscle. It's pretty much a few gym visits a week featuring the American Council on Exercise's recommended 30-45 minutes of cardio and some weights. Unlike ectomorphs, mesomorphs can do sets of 9–12 reps. They should also do chest presses, pull-ups, and lunges. Of course there are any number of exercises that can be switched around.

The exercises above are great, but since we're not kids anymore there are a few things we need to do physically whether we're interested in improving our bodies or not. What I'm talking about here is basic MIDMAN maintenance.

As I outlined at the top of the chapter, we are undergoing anatomical changes, none of which would be considered "improvements." Since we're stiffening up, clogging up and forgetting shit, we have to put some extra effort into stemming the tide of self-degradation. While the different body types have their own areas of focus, there is also a general need for a certain kind of exercise: old fuck exercise. Things like stretching and walking should be done because they serve an important purpose, not because they're what those hippy kids like to call "doing your thing." Do they work? You bet your bippy.

MIDMEN need to exercise, and not just to try and hang on to our good looks. The effects of exercise extend into every aspect of our lives. Exercise will help you maintain flexibility, increase energy, increase metabolism, strengthen bones, and help you sleep, not worry and be happy.

Hitting the gym to sweat on a treadmill or hoist weights may not be your preferred form of exercise. Maybe you'd prefer to take a speedy walk in a local park for 40 minutes. That's totally cool but you need to do it. Not doing so will make your guaranteed-to-suck-eventually life suck much sooner.

I do yoga. That's my "thing." Why, you ask? Well sir, for one thing yoga works the entire body. Most sports hit less than 20% of the body. Yoga gets to all four corners of your body (yes, in this example your body is perfectly square, making you wonderfully convenient to ship). Every organ, muscle and joint gets love when you do yoga. It also oxygenates the blood so you're actually more energetic after practicing than you were before. It's a cardiovascular and endocrine system workout. People of all sizes and types can do it. You just work it at your own rate, which will invariably increase as you practice regularly.

If you're not a gym guy, yoga offers another advantage; if you have enough room in your home you can just throw down a mat. I recommend the Jade Fusion Yoga and Pilates Mat; it's not cheap but it's thick and it lasts (I know, "That's what she said."). Several yoga studios have posted videos of their classes that you can do at home for about $15 a month. I use Yogisanonymous.com out of Santa Monica, CA, which has about a thousand videos streaming from a nice variety of teachers. Actually, practicing with decent teachers at your local gym or studio for at least a year is probably a good idea since they can correct you and help you develop good habits before your practice becomes a one-way video-based one.

Taking care of your body is about so much more than appearance. It's about avoiding interaction with any or all health practitioners! You don't want to let yourself start requiring doctors unless you really have to. You can avoid all kinds of heart disease, diabetes, whatever, if you watch your ass. Don't get me wrong; if the health care system weren't so fucked up there would be any number of disorders for which I might enjoy being treated. Some things, like appendectomies, can't be avoided. Actually, I had one but it was elective. I've always hated my appendix. It didn't do a fucking thing, just hung around freeloading in my body. Fuck you, get out! Needless to say, my spleen is on notice.

As I mentioned at the top of the chapter, aging is taking place in your body at the cellular level. This means that no matter how hard you try, shit will go wrong. Why not mitigate or delay the shitstorm? Here are a couple of key areas that you can work on to keep the ravages of remaining alive at bay:

1. Nature only puts a 40-year warranty on your back. I'm 55, my back goes out; *I* don't even go out! I had a bulging disc that, once I corrected it with yoga, left me with a very painful case of some rare neuropathy-like nerve horror in my right leg called PTH. Anything that touched the leg caused severe pain, so I continued doing the yoga but in my underwear so nothing would touch the leg (don't picture it; why should we both suffer?). The pain finally stopped, but the yoga didn't. I've been doing yoga now for about eight years and I have no intention of stopping. No single thing I can do for myself offers as much benefit. If you get nothing else from this book, take the yoga tip.
2. Sleeping well really matters. A few years ago Harvard published the results of studies that prove how much sleeping a sufficient amount impacts not just your looks, but your physical well-being. They claim 75% of us don't sleep enough at least a few nights each week. Granted, the study was conducted with women, but our stats can't be that far off. Here are a few of their reported effects of chronic sleep loss:
   - Health problems like weight gain, high blood pressure and decreased immune system functioning.

- Learning and memory deficiencies. People who slept after learning a task did better on tests later.
- Safety. If you're walking around all drowsy, you're at a much higher risk of falling, or in the case of famously sleep-deprived doctors, medical errors (wait, doctors conducted this study. I hope they were well-rested or all this info is crap).
- Mood. Sleep loss can make you act like an asshole. It can also stop you from pursuing stuff you enjoy.
- Cardiovascular health. Quoting Harvard's study, "Serious sleep disorders have been linked to hypertension, increased stress hormone levels, and irregular heartbeat." That's some shit right there.
- Disease. Immune function suffers to the extent that sufficient sleep may actually help fight cancer.

If you take care of your body, your body will take of you. You'll feel better and you'll look better. Even if you eat right and exercise you're still a MIDMAN so you'll probably still need a friendly assist from the next section.

GROOMING

Okay, now we're in my wheelhouse. I don't just groom, I MIDMAN groom. My concentration is less on trying to reverse the clock and more on trying to hang on to what I can. I'm playing the long con. Since I would be considered by general standards to be well-groomed but not obsessively fastidious, I may be able to present myself as a fair model.

In 2013, Braun, a leading razor manufacturer, conducted a study of British men. They found that *manscaping* to boost their body confidence is on the rise. More than 70% of those surveyed manscape.

Almost half do it for confidence and about 25% do it for their partners. Another 5% do it just so they can justify bathing in aftershave.

Take a look at your legs, arms, chest, ass, etc. Are you a Sasquatch? Do you look like you should have a zipper down your back? You may be a touch hairier than you need to be. A little snippy snip in the right places could actually shave off a few years.

In case you're self-conscious about harvesting your body's protein crop (holy shit, another inadvertent masturbation joke!), think about this; the box for the Philips Norelco Multigroom Pro Trimmer (there are Westminster Dog Show winners with shorter names than that) describes the clipper as being for "head to toe styling," so we can assume the trend has passed the tipping point. And style your body hair?! If you can *style* it, you've already let it go way too far. An ass pompadour is attractive to no one.

I want to make it clear that if you are in a relationship, any trimming you do or don't do should be the result of a frank conversation with your partner. It's something you want to agree on. If you've never broached this subject with your partner before, then the discussion itself will draw you closer. A relationship that is enduring even mild strain could only benefit by this kind of gesture of consideration. In essence you're saying, "I am willing to change my habits for you," which is pretty damn honorable. The conversation could go like this:

HUSBAND

(enters room stark naked) Honey? I know I haven't been paying a lot of attention to my grooming for the last 17 or so years and I thought you and I could have a conversation about how I can make myself look more attractive to you.

WIFE

What the fuck? You can start by putting something on; someone might see you and puke.

HUSBAND

You're the only one home.

WIFE

I meant me! You want to talk to me about grooming now? What, are you going to go get yourself a fucking Brazilian wax job? Wait; are you coming out to me?! OH-MY-GOD you're *gay*!

Okay, so maybe you'll just want to use your judgment and adapt the appropriate grooming suggestions on your own.

Since there's *so* much upkeep required to keep even a fit MIDMAN's body properly groomed, I'll start from the bottom and work my way up.

FEET: My wife has a little term she likes to use when I get dry, ridged calluses on my heels: caveman feet. She finds it disgusting. The calluses themselves are harmless enough; in fact I think they're kind of fascinating. They're composed of derivatives of the stratum corneum, which is dead tissue. It's the same material that comprises finger and toenails, whale baleen, hoofs, armadillo skin and snake rattles. But like mine, your significant other may not take to the naturally occurring miracle of foot protection you're walking around on. If you don't have a significant other currently, I'd lay odds that someone newly introduced to your feet would enjoy meeting them more if those feet were evolved at least to Neanderthal.

So, how do we coax the crusty crap off our heels? We just indulge regularly in two simple practices.

1. Pumice stone. When the gas-rich froth of glassy lava cools quickly – in thousands of years instead of millions – it forms into a light, porous rock. That's basically what pumice is. It's kind of a natural sandpaper and is used pretty much the same way. This is the same shit they put in mechanic's soaps

like Lava because it makes it abrasive enough to get oil and grease off. Get yourself a pumice stone at any drug store (get a good one) and put it in your shower. Then while you're conditioning your hair (and you *will* be conditioning your hair, Sonny Jim), sand down your heels and any other part of your foot that's getting a little too *One Million Years BC*. If you're working serious man-hoof, don't try and sand it all down at once, spread it out over several showers. Also, soaping up the foot seems to make the whole thing... better.

2. Apply balm. There are plenty of brands and types of callous-softening goo out there. Salicylic acid lotion is a well-known treatment for calluses. It can also help with warts, acne, and psoriasis. It works by swelling, softening and eventually removing excess skin. But it might be overkill and at certain strengths requires a prescription.

   Balms with olive oil, beeswax and usually some fancy tea tree oil, honey or unicorn tears are available at all the same places where they sell the pumice stone, so you can pick some up while you're there.

Toenails need to be trimmed and the linty paste needs to be scraped out from under the big toenails. Do it outside or over a trash-can, which the clippings will fly past 90% of the time. Think of this exercise less as grooming and more as sock preservation.

HAIRY LEGS: Let me be clear. I am not suggesting you shave your legs like the guys shrink-wrapped in neoprene and Italian logos we see speeding by on high-tech bicycles. In their case it makes sense; they want to have less wind resistance, so they shave themselves smooth and oil up. That's totally macho, the leg shaving and oil and stuff. I do tend to get a little suspicious when a fat guy does it. Seriously, man, you're built like Jack fucking Black and you figure it's that *leg hair* that's undermining your aerodynamics? Personally,

I think those guys just get their jollies packing their junk in spandex and taking it out for a joy ride. But this isn't about them, this is about you, unless I just described you, in which case I would like to speak on behalf of pretty much everyone on Earth and beg you to put on some cargo shorts.

Modern hair trimmers come with clip-on ends that allow you to set the length you want. This means you can actually trim your legs down to a more youthful hair length but not shave them all the way to Tour de France. It's especially important to trim your legs if you trim your chest and back, which I'll get to as we work our way northward. If you don't, you'll be all shorn on top and from the waist down you'll look like a satyr. The *Pan* look hasn't been in vogue since 100 BC.

Since the term "leg man" kind of means "ass man," I'll cover your ass in this section too. I don't mean, *cover your ass*, as in look out for you, I mean I will talk about your hairy ass right here and now.

From what I can gather from my journeys around the Net, women are cool with male body hair, just not too much of it. This particular field of study is the only one I have found where the word "taint" is commonly used parlance. The taint, on the outside chance you don't know, is the small area of flesh between the anus and the scrotum (I don't know why but that somehow sounds grosser than just saying between the ass and balls). The derivation of the word is shorthand for "It *ain't* your balls and it *ain't* your ass."

Women who are otherwise happy with some body hair really don't seem to like it much when it sprouts from the genitals and intimately surrounding areas. So my advice is trim everywhere, including the pubes, to a nice tidy length but totally shave the active duty forces. This means the full junk trio and the taint.

The entire ass can go hairless as well. One woman I found in a forum reported wanting to grab a handful of her man's ass in the heat of passion but she was snapped out of her reverie when he screamed holy murder because his hair was being ripped out. So shaving your ass *in toto* may be the way to go. I will admit right now that I shave my ass. I use an electric clipper on a really close setting, not a razor. I did it a couple of days ago and I probably need to do it again. Right now my ass actually has a five o'clock shadow. If I stuck a cigarette in my ass right now it would look like Humphrey Bogart in *The Treasure of the Sierra Madre*.

My personal technique for shaving the busiest intersection in town is to make sure my subjects are clean and very dry, and lightly shave with a freshly bladed, modern razor. Currently I use a Gillette ProGlide, but I don't think it matters. What does matter is that you pull your skin completely smooth before pulling the razor across it. You should also barely apply any pressure at all; the blades should do a fine job on their own. If you nick yourself, don't freak out—it's just skin. If you circumcise yourself, you probably need to slow down.

Manscaping, paired with some exercise and a little dietary tweaking, could only stand to place you in better stead in the pursuit of what matters. Imagine entering into any challenge feeling healthy and strong and displaying the kind of confidence that only comes from knowing that your balls are fresh, clean and as bald as a buzzard's skull.

BACK HAIR: Don't like it. Never did. Women don't tend to like it either. It's probably their least favorite man hair. Many a lady would climb a mountain of taint hair before so much as touching a single strand of back hair. There are three ways to deal with it:

1. **Don't deal with it**.
2. **Shave it.** Shaving it can be very easy or very hard depending on how close a shave you desire. If you don't mind going electric, the Mangroomer is a battery powered electric clipper on a long, bendable arm. This allows you to reach behind you and hit all the spots that time forgot.

The other way to shave is to shave, like with a razor. However, unless you're Plastic Man you can't shave your own back entirely. There are places on our bodies that nature just doesn't want us touching (you did the masturbation joke thing again). This means you need a friend to shave you. Do you have a friend to shave you? Is there anyone you could call? It's a pretty big favor to ask, I think. My wife has actually shaved my back several times, but not because I wanted her to. Actually, it was in the course of preparing me for the second method of getting the hair off of the back.

3. **Laser it.** Here's the deal, there are lasers that are used to kill hair follicles. Women use them on their hoohas and yes, I'll say it, their *taints*! They also do their armpits, mustaches, and even entire legs. Those same lasers work perfectly well on hairy man back. The process is pretty easy. First you get someone to shave your back. Ask a stranger, make a friend. Hire one of the guys from in front of Home Depot. Check yourself into your local gothic insane asylum and start a louse epidemic, anything; just get yourself shaved. Or just do what you can on your own; the laser joint will get the parts you couldn't reach before they commence to zapping.

   The treatment is really nothing. You go in, take off your shirt, lie on a table, and an RN draws a grid on your back and shoots a laser at you at close range for about 20 minutes. The laser is bright so you have to wear special glasses. The treatment feels like a rubber band snapping over and over, all over your back. The pain is totally manageable and is largely masked by a gust of cold air that accompanies each zap. Six treatments would cost you about $1,000 if you find a deal and there *are* deals. Six could do the trick, or it might take a few more depending on the density of your pelt.

CHEST HAIR: We all watched in horror as Steve Carell submitted himself to chest waxing in the film *The 40-Year-Old Virgin*. Guys actually do that to themselves. Weightlifters, dandies, fops and people like that. If you want my ten cents worth, I'm against it. For one thing, women don't hate chest hair, you just can't be Borat. So break out those clippers. Again, you'll have to choose the spacing attachment that brings it to a length you like, but totally shaven doesn't work because you're not really totally shaved and too short looks freshly shaved, which may not be cool either. You need some length, maybe half an inch. Also, by keeping hair shorter in some areas than others you can give the subliminal appearance of youth. Go shorter throughout the chest, but leave a touch more length in the area frisky bar girls like to call the "happy trail," which runs from your belly button south.

This pretty much takes you down to the bottom of your stomach or the top of your dick, depending how you look at it. Either way, it's your pubic hair. Some guys shave it off completely. I'm not comfortable with that. I see a conservative tuft of pubes in much the same way I see clean underwear; if I get in an accident, I won't be self-conscious. Now that I think of it, if I get in an accident, I may not be conscious, self or otherwise! But when I come to, I'd like to know I don't have the crotch of an 11-year-old boy under my surgical gown. So I keep 'em trim but not shaved.

Another much-heralded bonus from proper junkyard trimming is that Robin and the Two Hoods stand out nicely. By cutting back the hedges, you expose more real estate, which is cool no matter how big the lot is.

ARMPITS: Just a little trim with the clippers and you're good to go.

BACK OF NECK: Clippers often, razor sometimes. You can pull this off gentle and dry also.

EARS AND NOSE: Get yourself an electric nose and ear hair clipper and use it often! You really don't want to be hanging around with hair shooting out of your nose and ears like a lynx. If you don't already clip your nose hair, *what*?! This isn't just an aesthetic thing; you aren't getting all the air you could be getting. And stuff is getting stuck all up in there. Some guys remedy this by picking, which is the easiest way possible to make yourself look like a knuckle-dragging goon. Fuck, this whole subject is gross. I don't want to talk about it anymore.

FACE: There are a million ways to deal with facial hair. Right now beards are in style, or it took me too long to finish this book and they're not anymore. But if you're going with scruff or a short beard, remember to keep your lines clean but obscured. Definitive shave lines don't look as casual and unaffected as a gradual change in length. For instance, in my case I shave my neck on the closest clipper setting, the underside of my jaw on two and the facial beard on three. I shave the small area just above the beard and below the cheekbones with my regular blade razor to give it a nice neat line.

EYES: There are a couple of areas of the face that project more about us than others. At the top of that list, and coincidentally at the top of the face itself, are the eyes. That the eyes are the windows to the soul may be so, but they're also the clearest window to our lifestyle and stress level. The first impression we make on others is heavily reliant on our eyes. If we look hangdog and beaten, that's how we'll be perceived even if our minds are bursting with creativity and ambition. However, if we look alert, well-rested and healthy, people will want to work with us, work for us or hire us to work for them.

People wrinkle and age at different rates for different reasons. There's heredity and genetics, there's lifestyle and there's environment. Smile lines caused by smiling are great, but worry lines and dark under-eye bagging can tell a sad story (even if it's about a very happy night before). In keeping with the philosophy of the book, we're going to need those eyes for a few more years, so maintaining them matters.

We've all looked like shit, agreed? Waking up after too much indulgence and too little sleep is usually the perfect scenario for looking shitty. And what feature of the face takes the most brutal beating as a result of our bacchanal? That's right, *the glazzies, my droogie bratty;** the eyes. To mitigate our eyes' tell-tale signs of having been ridden hard and put away wet, we have to deal with the whole eye area.

Those nasty, bagging, dark circles under your eyes are the most obvious eye problem and are caused by fluid accumulation or edema. This can be caused by a number of things, including too much salt, allergies, dehydration, stress or being punched squarely in the nose.

Dark circles can be hereditary. If they are and you have the means and/or the desire, you can fight back. For about $1500 a doctor can treat the area with a fraxel laser. It's painless, takes about 15 minutes per eye, and it works. It even gives a little lift to the surrounding area.

The best possible way to maintain the eyes is with proper rest and nutrition. Sorry. Truth be told, though a wild night-before may provide you with your own personal *Día de Muertos,* if you're living well you'll snap back after your next good night's sleep.

The sun is the prime culprit in any facial aging scenario, including dark circles under the eyes. I, for one, choose not to fight the signs of aging by denying myself sun exposure. Being out in the sunshine is one of the things about life I love most, so I'm going to have to accept that it will age me and try to combat the symptoms through other means.

Sunscreens are a smart way to go, of course, but they aren't foolproof. They have to be applied at least 30 minutes before exposure and the best stuff has UVA, UVB and infrared protection. From what I gather from the experts, anything higher than 30 SPF is a waste. Also, reapplying could be

---

* Any *nadsat*, speakers out there?

an act of futility (or just an excuse to rub down your entire body in public). If you're stuck out there, do it every couple of hours anyway.

There are cosmetic products for dark eye circles on the market, like Men's Expert Hydra-Energetics by L'Oreal, which according to the company uses a "Peptide-Complex with Vitamin C and caffeine to help reduce the look of dark circles." I actually have the stuff and it does work for me. I guess caffeine *is* a real eye opener!

Bloodshot eyes are caused by your eyes being dry, whether it's from dehydration caused by alcohol intake or weed. Pollution and allergens like pollen in the air can also red things up real good. "Tear" formula eye drops can help.

I also use some kind of lotion on my face, especially around the eyes. There are some great products out there—and not only to moisturize, but to remove signs of aging and wear with ingredients like Retin-A. If you shop around for them online you're sure to see lots of pictures of women far too young to have had wrinkles removed.

Now, about that adequate rest thing. The eyes are only one of the countless facets of your health and appearance that benefit from a proper amount of rest. The Dalai Lama said, "Sleep is the best meditation," or I think that's what he said. His speeches put me out like a light. Everything is good about getting enough sleep. Luckily, the same steps you may need to take to access what truly matters to you could also pave the way to better sleep.

TEETH: I believe that somewhere in the haze of my writing mania I mentioned still having all my own teeth? Well, I do. Granted, a few are covered in crowns, but that just means they're dental royalty. Proper oral care is more important than we might think. A bum tooth is just the first domino to fall in a series of dominos that will result in great pain and expense. It all starts with an excruciating toothache. They always occur on the Friday night that begins a three-day dentist-free weekend. After sucking on Orajel for three days, you finally get to see the dentist. Now the meter is running, so get your wallet out. You're too far gone for the dentist to work on you before the teeth are cleaned, so they're getting cleaned. The dental hygienist is a lovely woman with an endearing accent from a country you can't identify. She approaches cautiously, fortified behind gloves, smock, two layers of mask, surgical cap, and glasses with dental loupes. You can only see her grotesquely magnified eyes and they reveal deep resentment. It's as if she'd loaned you *her* teeth and you totally fucked them up. She reaps her revenge during the cleaning as you cringe like Dustin Hoffman in *Marathon Man* screaming, "It's safe!" She finishes and proffers some floss, while whining plaintively, "Please." Then the X-ray dude comes in and it's "No worries," and "It's all good" for 15 minutes while he positions hard plastic paddles in your still toothachy mouth. Visitor number three comes in and lays out Dr. Torquemada, DDS's instruments of cavital persuasion. After you get to consider those for another ten minutes, in bursts your dentist. Like the hygienist, he behaves as if they were his teeth you so heinously neglected. "We've got some serious problem, here," he laments empathetically, while scrutinizing the X-rays. He'll stuff a temp into your emergency hole today, but it's only temporary and it's just the beginning. Words like crowns, implants, and root canal pepper his patter as he gusts out the door. And so the dominoes fall and the wallet empties.

Since that's not a world we want to visit, we have to take precautions. If you're already taking care of yourself orally (wow, *that* paints a nasty picture!) you can disregard this chapter, but if you've been lazy, take heed. The American Dental Association actually has special instructions for adults 40-60. They report that the average adult between 20 and 64 has three or more decayed or missing teeth. We all have a friend whose exhale smells like a chunk of pepperoni putrefying in the desert sun. That would be a tooth or teeth rotting in their head. If you have sensitivity or pain or an awareness of any disturbance all up in your grill, you may be unknowingly emitting a fetid stench yourself. Preventing or reversing such a fate is totally doable. There are two simple steps and you already know them.

1. *Brush twice a day*. They recommend changing your toothbrush every three or four months. I recommend switching to something like the Braun Oral-B electric but keeping a brush around for when you don't feel like powering up.
2. *Floss once a day*. I like the Johnson and Johnson's REACH mint waxed. If you don't floss you build up plaque, which hardens into calculus or tartar. It's just like "tartar" in tartar sauce in that your mouth will smell like fried clams, so lose it!

Bonus: Waterpik. There are a number of reasons why teeth can begin to separate: gum disease, nighttime grinding, fingernail chewing or just willful defiance. Or they just do. You could get braces or a retainer or a night guard, which is what I use to stop my grinding. If your teeth are a little separated you get little gaps between them that catch food. I don't mean the big Elton John front tooth gaps (which in French are called "*dents du bonheur*," or "lucky teeth" for some bizarre reason), just little ones. You'd think that flossing and brushing would empty all the crap out of those gaps, but don't bet on it. If you've been eating say, popcorn, and you floss then brush then waterpik, you will be amazed at the silo of cornhusks that come rinsing out.

Double bonus: Tongue scrapers! I know it's not teeth specifically, but it is oral hygiene and it does matter. You can buy a tongue scraper pretty much anywhere toothpaste is sold or you can use a tablespoon. Essentially, what you're doing is scraping the white crap off of your tongue. Why? Because that white crap is formed by oral bacteria and produces bad breath. Why? Because removing the thick coat of bacteria over your taste buds exposes them to things like "tasty stuff." Why? Because if you don't remove those bacteria and oral toxins your body will just reabsorb them and that's disgusting. Removing that white crap also boosts your immune system. That's why.

EYEBROWS: Whether your eyebrows are thick or thin, they grow. Really long eyebrows give the effect of the wearer being unkempt or worse, professorial. There are a lot of aging signs we can't do much about, but looking like Commander McBragg isn't one of them.

Trimming the eyebrows is pretty easy stuff; if you have hair-cutting scissors or an electric trimmer and a regular old fashioned pocket comb, you're in business. "Tapering" is the term in barbering for what you'll be doing here. Tapering means you take the comb and comb into the hair and clip what sticks out over the teeth. In this case, you're just putting the comb's teeth behind the eyebrows, against the brow, and snipping the hairs that stick out through the teeth. Your eyebrows, and therefore more facial real estate, will look better if you do this.

HAIR: If you have a great head of hair, well la-de-fucking-da. How nice for you. Many MIDMEN consider their hair the bane of their existence and I am among them. The history of my hair and what I've done to either preserve or replace it is a long and tragic one, though it does have a sort of happy ending.

I began losing hair in my early 20s, which is just not fair. My stand-up career was just getting started so I decided I would deal with it before anyone really noticed. Below I will share my journey.

HAIRPIECES. My first hairpiece was a throw rug that was actually sutured to my scalp. I don't want to say this thing was bad, but it actually had the word "Welcome" in the middle of it. I still have the scars... but not the rug. The hairpieces that followed were of much better quality; not human hair, but good. Because I was young and expected to have a full head of hair the effect was convincing. I did a couple dozen TV shows back in the 80s and early 90s, all of them wearing an all-but-undetectable piece. But the meticulous application and constant self-consciousness was driving me crazy.

TRANSPLANTS. When hair transplants made their move from "plugs" to "micrografts," I dug in. After several extremely painful transplant procedures, I had harvested and rearranged all that my head would allow. Today I have hair on my head. I designed my own receding hairline, so the look is age appropriate. I'm also still bald at the crown, or as my surgeon calls it, "the black hole," because no one has enough donor hair to fill it. I also have sizable "smile" scarring across the back of my head, or donor area. My hair easily hides it but the shaved head look is no longer an option for me.

The way transplants work is pretty simple. A doctor literally scalps a strip from your head in the area extending across the back from ear to ear. This is the area where male pattern baldness balds us last so the follicles are genetically predetermined to hang around the longest. Then the strip is segmented into individual follicles by a team of small Guatemalan women. Once that's done, the doctor pokes a hole in your head for each of the follicles and the women spend a few hours hand planting the follicles into the new holes. While they're working, you're sitting there dazed on Valium and Vicodin watching a movie and chatting with the Guatemalans, who are perfectly good company. The painful part is the administration of the Novocain, which requires a couple dozen injections all over your scalp. No bueno!

There is a new harvesting technique where the follicles are removed individually and transported to a new spot, which I assume would prevent the big scars, and even talk of cloning. Your continued research may send you in that direction, but I for one am done.

LASER. Every morning while I check my emails and the news on the Net (coughing into hand, "*look at porn*"), I run a laser light across my scalp. The light stimulates the follicles that haven't totally died yet and gets them to sprout anew. I have been pretty successful in reinforcing my transplanted hair with new growth from the lasers and I recommend them highly. There is a weird feeling you get, not pain, just weird, when the light connects with a viable follicle. My HairMax by Lasercomb seems to deliver more of those than my HairYes brand. I would strongly suggest trying this before succumbing to transplants since it's much less expensive, less painful and leaves no scars. If you're in the younger MIDMAN range, I recommend getting to it sooner than later as it will preserve what you have while restoring some of what you've already lost. Getting results requires persistence and time so stick with it.

PROPECIA. Brief history. The year was 1974. The place was the Dominican Republic. A guy named McGinley found that a group of male children all had an enzyme 5-alpha-reductase deficiency and we all know how that can be (?). Meanwhile, as a result of that they all had small prostates, zero hair loss and no acne. I don't know how McGinley gained access to all those kids' prostates, but life is strange in the islands. A compound called Finasteride was proven to create the same effect those young men were enjoying naturally. Originally released as Proscar to inhibit prostate growth, Propecia was released to take advantage of its hair preserving and growing qualities.

One of the reported side effects of Propecia is a loss in sexual drive. Of course guys who are losing their hair may also be reaching an age where they are experiencing a loss in sexual drive naturally, so it's hard to tell what's going on! I tried the stuff and, while correlation does not imply causality, I chose to blame it for my reduced sex drive and stopped. I don't recall my sex drive experiencing a slam-bam comeback, so use your own judgment.

BIOTIN. This is also known as vitamin H, even though it's a B vitamin. WTF? The list of uses for Biotin reads like a snake oil salesman's set list, but preventing hair loss is on it. You can take it as a supplement

(I do) or buy thickening shampoos and conditions that have it (I do that, too).

MENOXIDIL. Rogaine. Apply it twice a day, once in the morning and once at night and studies say you will retain your hair and even grow back some of what you've lost. It was originally released as some greasy lotion but now it's available in mousse form. I use it but since I also use biotin, lasers and have transplants; I don't know what the fuck is going on up there. However, Costco makes a Kirkland brand that costs so little, I figure what the hell.

HAIRCUT. Your haircut is the second most important component of your look, behind hair volume. Some people find the Bruce Willis chrome dome look very attractive and some find short cropped hair to be what they need. You can be very creative with whatever hairs you have but DO NOT go with the full-on Donald Trump hairchitecture (that warning was included on the outside chance Trump himself reads this book; no one else would do that).

SPRINKLY SHIT. Kind of a newish category. Toppik and Cabooki aren't just Manila's favorite comedy duo; they're two products that restore the look of a full head of hair a different way.

You may recall that back in the roarin' 90s, "operators are standing by" marketing pioneer Ron Popeil had a spray-on hair product? The idea was that the spray would paint your scalp the same color as your hair and everyone would be fooled into thinking you had hair. Yeah, but only the people who could also be fooled by the "got your nose" trick. My friend's bald dad used it and he looked like he had a freshly painted head. More amusing still was the lunar eclipse-shaped head paint design he left on the bathroom ceiling. Side note: like Sinatra in the world's worst rug, this guy somehow remained cool. That product is actually still available and it's called the GLH Hair System.

Toppik and Cabooki are both sprinkle-on as opposed to spray-on fillers. They both look and work about the same, though Toppik offers more color variety. If, like me, you're a bald spotter (meaning spotter of other guys' bald spots, not a guy with a bald spot, though my membership dues are paid up in both clubs), you may have taken notice of some of the obscured bald spots out there. I'll only cite *The Daily Show*'s Jon Stewart since he outted himself. Jon sometimes refers to his hair person's use of one of the aforementioned products to cover his thinning crown. The stuff actually works reasonably well, but in my opinion doesn't hold up under really close scrutiny in bright sunlight. It is perfect for catering halls where the kinds of, say, reunions where one may wish to look their most youthful might take place. But if you apply it wrong and get caught you could also look wonderfully desperate and pathetic.

The main difference between the two products is their content. Toppik uses primarily keratin taken from animal hair and Cabooki goes with 100% natural plant extract. I don't know how the animal hair was harvested, so I err on the side of plant-based.

Our bodies are the most important asset we the living have. Just because we can't actually see what's going on under our skin doesn't mean we don't have to act as a proper custodian for it if we want to continue to function. For me vanity was the inspiration, for you it might just be continuing to have a vessel that can watch TV and make alternating trips to the refrigerator and the bathroom. No matter what the reason, take care of yourself!

THE END

1. I'm actually getting old.

Every day, in every way, I am getting older. In a way this can be interpreted as good news. Getting older means getting closer to death and having that happen in the relatively near future couldn't be a better idea. Let's be real; the planet is fucked. MIDMEN may well be part of the final age group to tear a good one off of this bitch. Tell me you haven't thought about the advantage you have dying sooner than younger people. Anyone with half a mind can see that they're on their way into some kind of stark, arid, post-apocalyptic *Road Warrior*-planet shit. That is unless the human race can screech into a *SteveMcQueen-as-Bullitt-driving-a-1968-Ford-Mustang-390-GT2-+2-Fastback* U-turn and get serious about preserving this shit. MIDMEN would arguably be the most persuasive group to lead that charge, but I wouldn't hold what remains of my breathable breath. Notwithstanding our compassion and concern for those who will survive us, who wouldn't prefer to check out in the societal fashion to which we have become accustomed? Isn't it only right and just that those who live by the full stomach and comfortable furniture *die* by the full stomach and comfortable furniture?

MIDMEN who were born between 1950 and 1968 enjoyed some pretty sweet years to grow up in the western world. Yes, we're aging, but we listened to actual music. We had toys and got dirty outside. We got in trouble and won and lost. We got berated verbally and chased around the house by swinging father-fists while vicious threats were hurled at our escaping heels. I'm sorry, did I write that out loud? Life was different then than it is today and sure as hell different than it will be tomorrow. Our world wasn't perfect, but it was probably a better place to grow up.

The good news is that as times to get old go, this is a pretty cool time to get old (provided we die before the end of the world). One big difference for our generation is that we can get pretty incapacitated and still have some kind of life on the Internet. We're not growing old like *our* grandparents who were resigned to adjusting their rabbit ear antennas to get a clearer picture of *Hart to Hart* while waiting for their rotary phones to ring. On the Internet we don't age at all... because we can lie. The Internet allows us to research what we like, start a business or petition, blog, annoy politicians, communicate, network and create. If something motivates us, we can indulge in it and if we do, we will live longer and better.

2. It's ultimately going to suck.

I'm probably more afraid of 'near' the end than I am of the end itself. The fears start off pretty simply; I will get old physically. I will grow weaker and I will be infirm. I will have to stop driving. I will need to be taken care of like a baby. Help going to the bathroom. Having to be cleaned. If you ask an 80-year-old man wearing an adult diaper just how fast time went by since he was 50, he'd say, "Like that" and snap his fingers, breaking them instantly. There is a very bad time coming.

Worse, what if our minds stay sharp through it all? Maybe we'll have to just lie there having exciting ideas and thoughts and wishing we could make plans while our bodies are just shutting down all around us. Our vital systems will be failing one after another until we're not even people anymore, just occupied beds. Hospital time is a gimme. That's some scary shit; medical hardware banging around in the hallways all night, somebody groaning somewhere, and that someone might be me! Lying there, waiting. And for what? To leave? To return to what, a life of crushing leisure and pharmaceutical consumption? There's no cure for the disease of aging; it just gets worse.

Have you ever walked through a convalescent home or hospice care center? Not cool. The hallways are lined with what are basically the still-living remains of human beings. Makes one wonder if maybe we can live *too long*. But we're likely to hold out until the last possible second. It's in our DNA.

If we really allow ourselves to go into our personal dungeon of pain and honestly consider where things are headed, we may find that our own physical deterioration isn't really the scariest thing. There are two things that could be way more horrifying.

The first is that we won't be of any significance. No opinion, no say so, nobody. The second one is even worse; we're probably not going to die before everyone we love. If the people you know are dropping as fast as the people I know, then it's already too late for that. There is no clearer or more difficult way to understand that we are nothing without those we love than to lose them. Every time one goes we lose this chunk of our world. And one day, if we've been lucky enough to have one, we may lose that one person who makes the whole thing worthwhile. We lose our best friend, and there go most of the pieces. And if we're really old when it happens, platitudes like "Time heals all wounds" don't really apply to us anymore; we just have to drag what's left of ourselves around until we run the clock out.

3. Tough shit. I will still need to live life to the fullest until I can't anymore.

The intention of this book is to offer MIDMEN a route through their midlife crises. It's a frightening time, but it's temporary. Or at least it can be. However, if we don't find what matters to us and pursue it, we are doomed. A study by some economists in Switzerland, where the

Alpine valleys are black with economists, is among many studies that have proven that a reduction in the retirement age causes a significant increase in the risk of premature death for men. Premature is defined as death before age 67. Retirement shouldn't only be defined as no longer working at a *job*, it should be understood to mean a loss of direction, of *raison d'être*. But if we're involved in something that deeply motivates us, we live longer and better.

Okay, here's the big reveal; this book was actually all about me, but not in an autobiographical way. I'll explain. See, I have a long history of failure. This is my fourth book, just for starters. I have written six screenplays. I have created and/or produced numerous unsuccessful TV pilots and presentations for various networks and even the one that made it to air failed gloriously. My acting career topped out with a series of commercials for a phone company that failed and a Miller Beer commercial that I was literally fired from during the shoot, pretty much for sucking as an actor. I have also hosted TV pilots for networks and cable, and the only one that went to series went without me hosting. I made an elaborate period short about legendary French farter Le Petomane that qualified for Oscar contention and the 35mm print that went to the Academy for screening had a fucked up soundtrack. As a TV writer I've made it on to a few staffs, like the much-loved cartoon Rugrats, but never got the big career break to jump to long term, prime time network stuff. The stand-up thing went okay, I guess. However, if I hadn't moved into other areas I'd still be on the road slinging gags at comedy club goers half my age. I have been a qualified media failure. Given my history and the odds of any book succeeding in the larger sense, the writing of this book was an act of financial futility. It is to the failure born. So how does that make this a book about me? Because I fucking wrote it. I wrote it irrespective of its almost assured future in obscurity. I wrote this book because writing matters to me. I need to be in the process of writing. That's why I've also posted numerous, lengthy blogs about my imprudent travels around the world. For me, the blogs fueled the travel, not the other way around. I also have a stack of short stories, a pile of sitcom specs and on and on. I may have let my Writers Guild of America status shift to emeritus, but I am a writer.

As I wrote a couple of times earlier in this book, "It takes a long time to reach a worthy goal but only seconds to utter the words, 'I'm done.' This means you fucking well better enjoy the process of reaching that goal because that is how you spent your life." The quality of your work will likely have little or no bearing on the result's chance of success.

I had a screenplay distributed that earned me invites to literally every studio of note in Hollywood. It didn't sell. However, in the course of all of my near miss meetings I received some words of wisdom. The executive from one major studio who felt I deserved to sell the script said, "Just because you deserve something doesn't mean you're entitled to it." I loved writing that script and its failure to sell can't take that away from me. So, I understand that the success or failure of this book has absolutely no bearing on my enjoyment of writing it. It is safe to assume that if you are reading this book, I have already sucked up my few seconds proclaiming myself done and am on to writing something else. It's like those sewers in Farmingdale when I was a kid; there's no light at the end of the tunnel, just a series of lights as I move through. As Winston Churchill perfectly stated, "Success consists of going from failure to failure without loss of enthusiasm."

We all make decisions in our lives that will affect other decisions. If you decide to have children, you'll have to continue deciding on every aspect of their upbringing. If you decide to take out a mortgage and buy a house, you'll have to decide how to pay for it every month for 30 years. My wife and I have a non-writing oriented business and an office and responsibilities and everything, but I never forget that one of my most important responsibilities is to write. No matter what your "thing" is you need to make decisions that allow you to get you some. It's the conscious creation and maintenance of a radius that serves us. To pursue our bliss in life, regardless of how pointless, having a healthy body, an excited mind, and a strong foundation of support from those around us provides a huge leg up.

One accurate measurement for self-satisfaction is very simple to adopt; when we find ourselves breathing our last, will we be able to look back at a life we are proud of or at least satisfied with? If so, you rule. If not, we need to fill our lives with the things we won't regret looking back on! It is unlikely that reviewing a million hours of TV watching or a billion hours of video game playing will provide us with much pride in our final hours.

One way we can conduct a review of our lives objectively is to consider our eulogies. Unless you're very unpopular, *someone* is going to be eulogizing you *some*day. Would you be proud of what they'd have to work with or would you just cross your ghostly fingers and hope they lie? If your eulogy isn't shaping up to be a speech next to which you'd be proud to lie dead, it's a clear indication that you need to punch it up a little! And that means doing more shit you'll be proud to have done.

To assist you in finding out how you'll come out of your funeral looking, besides pale, I give you Midlibs – Eulogy Edition. Just go through the speech below and fill in the blanks with the suggested parts of speech. Good luck and Godspeed.

Today is a very (emotion) day because today we are gathered to say (interjection) to a (adjective) man who many of us (infinitive)ed. While (your name) won't be with us physically anymore, his memory will live on. Let us look back on his (superlative) life.

(Your name) was born in (city, state) in (year). As a child he was (adjective) and (adjective). His favorite pastime was to (verb). He proved himself to be a (speed) learner and (verb)ed at (hobby, skill). His skill at that early age would (define/not at all define) his future. (Your name) was a (adjective) student earning (A-F) s throughout his education.

His favorite toy as a child was a (toy) with a (color, accessory). He would take it to the (location) and play for (time period). He spent even more time with his best friend (person). The two shared a love of things like (authors, TV shows, celebrities, movies, Barbara Eden).

But grades notwithstanding, he made (adjective) use of his school years, gaining experience in (verb). His favorite teacher in grade school was (favorite teacher in grade school) who was cool because (he/she) would (verb) in the classroom.

His life at home with his sibling/s (person/s) was (adjective). If it weren't for (person/s) (noun) (your name) would never have been able to (verb) or (verb/w event).

(Your name) took his first job as a (occupation) at the age of (age), which led to more positions in (a different/the same) field. He went on to spend (years) of his life working as a (occupation), which he (infinitive)ed. In recent years he paid his bills by (verb and/or occupation. Note, 'mooching' is a verb *and* an occupation).

Romance came into (your name)'s life when he met his first (noun; girlfriend, wife, gay dude) at the age of (age). (Noun) was the apple of his (noun), and the relationship lasted (time frame or end date or 'until today'). (Repeat paragraph for each significant relationship).

(Your name) was father to (children's names or 'nobody and the tests confirmed it!'). (If applies) They will remember their father as (adjective, noun) who gave them (money, time, love, the cold shoulder, etc.). They are (here, not here or not here because they don't exist) today.

As I'm sure most of you know, (your name) had a (adjective) sense of humor. If I may, I'd like to share his favorite joke. (insert favorite joke)

We can all agree that the joke tells us a lot about him. But if there was one thing (your name) loved to do it was (verb). He could (verb) for hours until his (noun) was completely (adjective). Of course anyone who did that much (verb) is going to bear the evidence and (your name)'s body tells the tale. As he lies before us, his physical shape brings to mind (celebrity with the same body as you). And in that may we find solace.

Charity and kindness were (adjective) to him. They took up (period of time) in his life. His loss will bring (interjection) (adjective) to those who survive him.

In closing I would like to read something (your name) wrote. He (did/definitely didn't) ask that it be read at his funeral, (so/but) I'll read it (now/anyway). It's a (letter, screed, madman's ravings) for (name of logical recipient of final words).

"(Person), you have been my (adjective, noun). Whenever I thought about you, I felt (emotion). You taught me that I should (verb) and not be a (noun) like (different person). From you I learned that having a (noun) means nothing without (interjection). I am not a (adjective) man, but I am a man and when I pass I hope you will tell (person/s) and all of the other (adjective, person/s) that (your name) truly (infinitive)ed them. I only hope I have (verb)ed others even more than myself and leave behind a (adjective) world."

How did you make out? Were you left proud? Disgusted? Bored? Our job while we're alive should be to create the best eulogy we can and not stop creating it until we are totally immobilized.

If we play our cards right, we can delay the "It's ultimately going to suck" portion of our lives down to almost nothing. We could conceivably have a life that is painless and self-gratifying (your final easy masturbation joke) until we're a ripe old age. The best guidance we can hope for in our lives is to see to it that when the bell tolls for we, we can go out satisfied. If you are lying in your deathbed and the majority of your thoughts are upbeat and your outlook is defiantly sunny (yes, in this example, you're a dying Osmond), you are truly going out in style. You'd also be in the vast minority because most people fear death regardless of the lives they may have led.

In 1977 the *Book of Lists,* which ironically, is not on my list of books, asked 3,000 U.S. residents, "What are you most afraid of?" Death tied sickness for the number six position. Speaking before a group came in at number one which, of course, is ridiculous. That suggests someone would rather beg for the death penalty than defend himself in court or would find being chased by a grizzly less frightening than being pursued by a paying audience. I maintain that fear of death is ultimately number one. Well, fuck; our radiuses are already wrought with fear. Will our family negotiate their respective lives safely? Will my bills continue to be paid? Having a fear of death on top of it all could be a huge obstacle to our indulging in that special thing that matters to us – you know, the one you figured out earlier in the book, back before you started dieting, working out and shaving your ass. Remember?

No less than Sigmund Freud himself observed that midlife crisis was caused by our fear of our own mortality. If we didn't have that hanging over us, everything would be cool. But, no. We turned middle aged and one morning we woke up and realized how temporary it all is. Death is real, it's hanging around near us and it's checking its watch.

The only people who don't suffer from fear of death are people who have actually had near death experiences. In every piece of reportage I've read about near death experiences, everyone comes out of it having have an awesome, peaceful experience. Their vital signs zero out, their entire life flashes before their eyes, somebody revives them and they wake up a new zest for life, and no fear of death!

This book has gone to painstaking lengths to avoid any elements that might be described as New Age. And if at any point the content threatened to enrich you in a way that would have rendered you even remotely enlightened, the notion was immediately dispelled (yes, in this book you remain a little dick-having, drug cartel-running, tooth-sucking, perfectly square-shaped, dying Osmond). But now we're going there.

So, here's what we're going to do; we're going to take a minute right now and drop dead. Given the suicide stats for MIDMEN, that probably wasn't diplomatically stated. What I mean is we are going to attempt to approximate the act of dropping dead. Guided imagery is a basic practice for people who meditate. Essentially, it's story-telling. You close your eyes and your guide starts saying shit and you're supposed to envision it. The purpose more often than not is to relax the meditators and bring them to a mental space where they can approach life situations with an open mind.

During my one-man show *Life in the Middle Ages,* I would use this technique to lead the audience on a trip through the process of dying. It turned out to be way more effective than I could have predicted. The people who took the process seriously got a great deal out of it. Many of them came back to see the show again with friends, specifically for this experience. So, in spite of my inability to lull you with my sonorous voice, I am going to invite you to attempt to try and receive the same benefits in print. The upside of digging into this by reading instead of in a theater is you can take all the time you want... and no one will see you cry (most of the audience cried). If you're not in a place where you can concentrate, then you may want to save this for when you are. Seriously, find a nice quiet, dimly-lit room or shady spot outside where you are all but certain you won't be interrupted. If you're on the train or a plane, wait. It's pretty much the end of the book, so just put it aside and read a magazine until you're properly situated. If you're in the right place and you have plenty of time, cool.

Let's start by just taking a deep, relaxing breath. Fill your lungs all the way up and exhale very slowly. Let your shoulders hang loose.

Breathe into them; just let them go. Relax your eyes as much as you can while leaving them open enough to read. Take all the time you'd like to get nice and rubbery. Let your neck and shoulders go a little looser with every long exhale. Just breath for a while; no hurry. If your eyes are nice and relaxed then you can experiment with letting them softly close as you summon each of the memories that will be coming up. This will be a very cool experience, so there's no need for any tension at all. Three more deep breaths. Long inhales, even longer exhales. Slow down.

Okay, let's go back to remembering an early time in your life. Try to bring back the first memory you can. It could have been the view from a high chair or carriage, or a toy. Maybe it's somebody's giant face eclipsing your world. Maybe a pet? Really produce the images in your mind's eye. Take all the time you need.

Can you visualize your kindergarten classroom? The chunky toys? Your favorite toy? Take your time.

Maybe when you were really little you took a trip to someplace huge like a museum, or a zoo. Think about the sounds and smells. How huge everything looked. As you got just a little older, you may have taken trips into nature to camp or hike. Was there a lake? Do you remember swimming in the cold water? Did you scramble around along little trails? Try to feel it on your feet and your arms. Envision the people you were with, your parents or siblings, the way they looked then. Take a few extra moments to really go through them and see them. Maybe even hear them. Did they say something you remember? What were you wearing? Did you have a favorite piece of clothing? How did it feel on your skin?

Elementary school starts. Do you walk to school? Take the bus? Picture your desk, the chalkboard. Conjure the smell of Elmer's glue, Play Doe and school lunch food. Remember the lunch ladies? Close your eyes and picture every teacher you can. Slow down. Take all the time you need. How about your first best friend? Your wet raincoat on a rainy day.

Go on that trip to the amusement park. Feel the rides, smell the food. Feel the thrill.

Your eyes lock on your first crush. Hold this one for a little while. It's been a long time.

Now, grow up a little. New schools, changing classes. Picture your locker. Can you remember the combination? Try.

Your first car, your car friends. First ticket? Were you guilty?

Okay, here's a biggie; your first time having sex. If you'd like you can stay here for a second, or just zip ahead to your first *perfect* time.

Now you have your own place. Was it a dorm? An apartment or rented room? Did you have a roommate? Picture the front door. Remember your neighbors. What were your local stores? Your favorite pizza place.

Your job. How many jobs? Think about places, your responsibilities, co-workers, all those bosses. Try to picture the faces of as many past bosses as you can. No rushing.

Then maybe the career. Remember some of the highlights, the tough spots. Slow down and really feel the work. The long days. The clock you watched.

Remember something you won, maybe an award or a contest. How about something substantial that you lost? It could be a piece of jewelry or money on a bet.

You meet someone special. You commit for a while. Remember her face, her laugh, her smell. Maybe it wasn't a "her." Just summon the image as clearly as you can.

Maybe you meet someone else. Maybe a few other people and commit for a while. Sometimes a very, very short while. As with the teachers, stop and close your eyes for a while and produce the images of your past partners in your mind.

You finally grow up. You have bills and responsibilities. Are you married? Picture your wife as she looked when you met her. Maybe you have a kid or two or three. Remember their births. Slowly, very slowly, watch them grow up. Maybe watch them move away. Take time out here and really produce the sights, smells and sounds of your children as they grew.

Perhaps some others have come and gone from your life. And maybe somebody died. Grandparents? A neighbor? A close friend? A parent? Imagine all of their faces as clearly as you can. Their voices, their presence. Take your time.

Maybe you lost someone very close to you and your world changed, or maybe it's a friend from way back. See them vividly. Maybe it's a friend with four legs. Remember the names, what it was like to play with them; to sleep with them next to you.

Maybe you lose someone else. And someone else.

Now let go of all of the images you've summoned and just picture a soft white light small and far away. A peaceful, warm light, growing so slowly you can barely detect it as it comes toward you.

The light grows closer, and its warming glow surrounds you. Feel the subtle heat on your arms and face. Soak it in.

Our shoulder and face muscles surrender to the warmth of the light and totally let go. And now, right here, in our final moments, we see emerging from the soft glare of the light, all those who have passed before us. Grandparents and old friends even beloved pets long gone join them, all moving in peaceful slow motion. Smiling, their arms are outstretched and wrap you in an aura that whispers, "There is nothing to fear here; there is only love." And you believe them. You embrace them. Your cares dissolve, your worries disappear.

Take your time.

Feel the embraces.

See them.

Be with them.
See their smiles.
Still warmed by their presence you begin to back away.
Very slowly drifting back, keeping those good feelings.
You wave once more, but it's not good-bye, it's so long, because as long as they live on in your mind, you'll be back and you'll see them again and now you know it will be okay.
And you keep backing away. The light grows smaller and you can feel your world surrounding you.
And you can feel your mind acknowledging the now.
Every deep breath you take brings you closer to your new self; a self without fear of death, a self at peace with your past.
And you are back.

Okay, are you happy now; you died. Not so bad, right? If we can allow ourselves to accept this experience as our actually having died, then we can learn the most important lesson a MIDMAN can learn; nothing is that important. Had we truly died, the jobs we thought needed doing, the fears we thought needed fearing and the obligations we though needed obligating (?) would all vanish. They would dissolve into the ether like the release of our final breath. And everything would go on without us. Our lives post "death" are what I like to call, "Life in the Encores." It's already over and the rest is a bonus

Literally, as I wrote this very chapter, a comic I knew from the '80s passed away. Twelve days before, he was just a guy about my age out gigging. Out of nowhere, he contracted Guillain-Barré Syndrome and today he is gone. That could have just as easily been you or me.

If we ask an 80-year-old what he would have done more of had he known how fast his life would have passed, obviously he would tell us he would have spent more time indulging in the things made him laugh. As we learned from the Vitruvian man illustrations, aging will eventually rob us of all five of our senses. Our sight is probably already going, our hearing is next, then our smell, which means taste, and finally touch... but you *can* keep your sense of humor. If we create a radius that properly serves us, we can be happy and laugh right up until the moment we can't inhale enough to laugh again. We can laugh right in death's face right to the last joke. And people have proven this.

Groucho Marx' last words to his nurse when she asked if he was dying were, "Die, my dear? Why, that's the last thing I'd do!"

James French, was a murderer who got the chair in 1966. Before they hit the switch he turned to the reporters and said, "Hey, fellas! How about this for a headline for tomorrow's paper? 'French Fries'!"

Oscar Wilde was literally lying on his death bed and with his very last breath said, "Either the wall paper goes or I do." That's fucking funny!

Voltaire was lying on *his* death bed when someone asked him to renounce the devil. He snapped back, "Hey, this is no time to be making enemies!"

My favorite one took place back in 1854. Thirty thousand people turned out to see the hanging of a murderer named Dr. William Palmer. There he stood on the gallows, hands tied, noose around his neck. Before stepping on the trap door he gently tapped his foot on it and said, "Is this thing safe?"

Throwing our best one liner as our *last* one liner is unlikely to occur if we're not ending a life that has satisfied us. That can't happen if we haven't created a radius where the things that matter to us can thrive, or at least exist. If we MIDMAN-up, and are ballsy enough to confront the challenges that separate us from our true (read; not media created) desires, the Grim Reaper will have no choice but to give us a happy ending. (Not that kind. I think I'm done with you.)

Made in the USA
Middletown, DE
16 May 2018